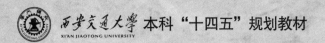

西安交通大学 本科"十四五"规划教材

体味西方礼仪

（第2版）

主编 刘 浩 董小红

编者 （按姓氏音序）

蔡 宁 董小红 刘 浩

邵 娟 许小艳 杨 扬

Savouring Western Etiquette
(the 2nd edition)

图书在版编目（CIP）数据

体味西方礼仪：汉文、英文 / 刘浩，董小红主编.
-- 2版. -- 西安：西安交通大学出版社，2024.8
ISBN 978-7-5693-2523-2

Ⅰ.①体… Ⅱ.①刘…②董… Ⅲ.①礼仪－西方国家－高等学校－教材－汉、英 Ⅳ.①K891.26

中国国家版本馆CIP数据核字（2023）第231453号

体味西方礼仪（第2版）
Savouring Western Etiquette (the 2nd edition)

主　　编	刘　浩　董小红
策划编辑	蔡乐芊
责任编辑	庞钧颖
责任校对	李　蕊
封面设计	任加盟
出版发行	西安交通大学出版社 （西安市兴庆南路1号　邮政编码710048）
网　　址	http://www.xjtupress.com
电　　话	（029）82668357　82667874（市场营销中心） （029）82668315（总编办）
传　　真	（029）82668280
印　　刷	陕西思维印务有限公司
开　　本	880mm×1230mm　1/16　印张　12.5　字数　356千字
版次印次	2024年8月第2版　2024年8月第1次印刷
书　　号	ISBN 978-7-5693-2523-2
定　　价	52.80元

如发现印装质量问题，请与本社市场营销中心联系调换。
订购热线：（029）82665248　（029）82667874
投稿热线：（029）82668531

版权所有　侵权必究

第 2 版前言
Preface to the 2nd Edition

《大学英语教学指南（2020 版）》（以下简称为《指南》）指出，"大学英语的教学目标是培养学生的英语应用能力，增强跨文化交际意识和交际能力，同时发展自主学习能力，提高综合文化素养，培养人文精神和思辨能力，使学生在学习、生活和未来工作中能够有效地使用英语满足国家、社会、学校和个人发展的需要。"《指南》在大学英语基础、提高、发展三个级别的教学要求中，都包括了对跨文化交际能力的描述，如提高目标要求"在与来自不同文化背景的人进行交流时，能够较好地应对与对方在文化和价值观等方面的差异，并能够根据交际需要较好地运用交际策略"。价值观是关于"标准"的抽象体系，它会以艺术的形式体现在戏剧、小说等之中，也会以具象的形式在人们的言谈举止中表现出来，礼仪不仅仅是指文明礼貌举止，还包括民族风俗、地域习惯、场合仪式等合乎社会公共道德的行为规范，也是一个社会群体的文化价值观的具体体现。在大学英语课程体系中开设西方礼仪文化这门课程，并不是简单地让学生了解西方社会中的行为礼仪，促进学生的跨文化交际能力，更重要的是使学生能够通过学习这些礼仪，探究礼仪之上的西方文化价值理念，并更深刻地了解中华文化和价值观。作为大学英语课程中一门拓展课的教材，在本教材的第 1 版使用了 12 年之后，编者根据最新的《指南》对其内容进行了部分调整，调整的宗旨在于通过学习西方礼仪，帮助学生洞察东西方文化的差异，从而提高跨文化交际的能力，同时通过分析、讨论等文化拓展练习，更好地了解中华文化的独特性，坚定文化自信。

鉴于此，第 2 版教材在第 1 版的基础上，整合了个别单元，将原来的 14 个单元压缩到 10 个单元，单元内容覆盖日常生活、工作、休闲娱乐等主要场合。同时，本版增加了 Introduction 和 Cultural Exploration 两部分。Introduction 以听力的形式，对该单元涉及的礼仪文化进行简单的引导；Cultural Exploration 部分则通过鉴赏、阅读、讨论等不同形式的练习，引导学生了解与本单元礼仪文化相关联的中华文化，加深学生对中华文化的理解，让学生更好地用英语传递礼仪中的中国故事，从而树立和提升民族自信心。此外，第 2 版对第 1 版中的部分案例和阅读文章进行了更换，阅读文章后也增加了阅读理解练习题，帮助学生更好地理解文章、抓住学习要点。

跨文化交际的基础在于对本文化和异文化的认知和了解，只有坚持平等、理解的原则才能做到不失去自我，达到共同理解。在教学过程中，教师可参考跨文化交际研究中的三个代表性理论：价值维度理论（Value Dimensions）、价值取向理论（Value Orientations）以及高语境与低语境理论（High-Context and Low-Context Orientations），以理论为指导，分析讨论文化差异问题及其成因。同时，建议教师注意引导学生思辨地看待礼仪文化差异，避免文化交流中的刻板印象（stereotype）及民族中心主义（ethnocentrism），培养学生尊重不同国家和民族礼仪文化的意识，使学生在了解西方文化的同时，更加热爱中华文化，秉持美美与共、差异并存的理念，帮助他们站在更高的地方看世界。

编　者

2024 年 3 月

第 1 版前言
Preface to the 1st Edition

《体味西方礼仪》是在西安交通大学出版社的精心策划下,由陕西省大学外语研究会组织,西安交通大学西方礼仪文化课程团队根据教育部颁布的《大学英语课程教学要求》(以下简称为《课程要求》)所编写,是一本主要面向非英语专业本科生的应用型语言文化类选修课教材。

编写依据

1.《体味西方礼仪》以《课程要求》为指导。本书全面贯彻《课程要求》精神,目的是"培养学生的英语综合应用能力,特别是听说能力,同时增强其自主学习能力,提高综合文化素养,以适应社会发展和国际交流的需要。

2.《体味西方礼仪》以现代外语教学理论为指导。将"以学生为中心的主题教育模式"引入课堂,关注学生的要求和兴趣,引导学生积极思考、主动参与。

3.《体味西方礼仪》充分考虑大学综合英语类课程的要求,并恰当与之衔接。经过综合英语的学习,学生已经达到《课程要求》的第一层次,即基本要求,所以在本书的编写过程中,编者以学生的第一层次语言能力和思辨能力为出发点,选择和处理编写材料。

教材特色

1. 编写体例独特。不同于传统教科书的编排结构与顺序,本书采用以操练和讨论为主的编排模式,通过有趣的课堂互动和讨论来学习理论知识。多样的课堂互动活动设计寓教于乐,激发学生的学习兴趣,创造轻松的学习环境。

2. 教学理念先进。教材编写充分考虑教学内容,采用创新的教学模式和教学方法,在提高学生语言能力的同时,提升跨文化素养。

3. 技能融合,综合培养。练习设计不仅关注学生英语语言技能的实践与运用,还重视其创新思维能力的培养,既帮助学生巩固语言基础,又进一步培养学生的实际应用能力,尤其是听说能力,从而帮助学生稳步提高英语语言水平。

教材构成

全书共分 14 个单元,每个单元讨论 1 个主题,每个主题包含 4 个部分,分别如下:

Part I Check Your Manners，以判断或选择的练习形式测试学习者对本单元礼仪知识的了解程度。

Part II Practice，以不同的互动练习模式，在操练中进一步学习和掌握礼仪知识点。

Part III Case Study，以案例分析的形式，分析礼仪所承载的文化问题，探讨不同文化中礼仪所带来的文化差异问题。

Part IV Reading for Etiquette Tips，以阅读理解的模式，汇总和复习本单元所涉及的西方礼仪文化。

教学建议

《体味西方礼仪》是一门文化类选修课的教材，使用本教材时，重点应该从培养学生语言基础知识和能力转变为拓展知识、了解世界文化的素质教育，在课程教学过程中应当充分考虑培养学生的文化素质和跨文化交际能力。

针对本教材内容，建议课堂教学以互动形式为主，学生就教学内容进行模拟操练，并根据已有的知识互相点评，教师作最后总结。如果教师能提前准备相关道具，增加知识性和趣味性，教学效果会更好。

由于各校教学条件及学生英语水平的差异，建议教师可根据本校实际采用适当的教学方法，将教材内容合理安排为课堂授课与课下自习部分。

本书的编写得到了西安交通大学出版社的大力支持，杜瑞清教授、杨跃教授、黄平安教授等专家多次听取编写汇报，详细审阅稿件。编辑黄炜炜对本书的出版也付出了大量的心血。另外，我们在编写过程中，参考了许多国内外的图书资料和网站文章，在此向原作者表示衷心感谢！

本书虽经反复讨论和精心编写，但经验不足，水平有限，衷心希望广大师生和读者不吝指教。

编　者

2010 年 8 月

目　录
Contents

Unit 1　Visiting a Friend 1

　　Section 1　Introduction 2

　　Section 2　Check Your Manners 2

　　Section 3　Practice 3

　　Section 4　Case Study 6

　　Section 5　Reading for Etiquette Tips 7

　　Section 6　Cultural Exploration 14

Unit 2　Hosting the Home Guests 17

　　Section 1　Introduction 18

　　Section 2　Check Your Manners 18

　　Section 3　Practice 19

　　Section 4　Case Study 22

　　Section 5　Reading for Etiquette Tips 24

　　Section 6　Cultural Exploration 32

Unit 3　Dining Culture 35

　　Section 1　Introduction 36

　　Section 2　Check Your Manners 36

　　Section 3　Practice 37

Section 4	Case Study	39
Section 5	Reading for Etiquette Tips	42
Section 6	Cultural Exploration	48

Unit 4 Behaving in Academic Situations ... 51

Section 1	Introduction	52
Section 2	Check Your Manners	52
Section 3	Practice	54
Section 4	Case Study	58
Section 5	Reading for Etiquette Tips	61
Section 6	Cultural Exploration	68

Unit 5 Making Telephone Calls ... 71

Section 1	Introduction	72
Section 2	Check Your Manners	72
Section 3	Practice	74
Section 4	Case Study	78
Section 5	Reading for Etiquette Tips	81
Section 6	Cultural Exploration	89

Unit 6 Interviewing ... 93

Section 1	Introduction	94
Section 2	Check Your Manners	94
Section 3	Practice	95
Section 4	Case Study	101
Section 5	Reading for Etiquette Tips	105
Section 6	Cultural Exploration	111

Unit 7 Working at the Office 113

Section 1 Introduction 114
Section 2 Check Your Manners 114
Section 3 Practice 116
Section 4 Case Study 117
Section 5 Reading for Etiquette Tips 120
Section 6 Cultural Exploration 127

Unit 8 Meeting Business Partners 129

Section 1 Introduction 130
Section 2 Check Your Manners 130
Section 3 Practice 132
Section 4 Case Study 135
Section 5 Reading for Etiquette Tips 138
Section 6 Cultural Exploration 147

Unit 9 Attending a Wedding Ceremony 149

Section 1 Introduction 150
Section 2 Check Your Manners 150
Section 3 Practice 151
Section 4 Case Study 155
Section 5 Reading for Etiquette Tips 159
Section 6 Cultural Exploration 164

Unit 10 Touring Abroad and Leisure Time 167

Section 1 Introduction 168
Section 2 Check Your Manners 168

Section 3　Practice 169

Section 4　Case Study 172

Section 5　Reading for Etiquette Tips 175

Section 6　Cultural Exploration 184

Bibliography 187

Unit 1
Visiting a Friend

You will learn in this unit
- ☐ different ways of greeting
- ☐ gift etiquette
- ☐ visiting etiquette
- ☐ thank-you note

SECTION 1 INTRODUCTION

🎧 **Listen to the following passage and fill in the blanks.**

Problems of communication typically arise when persons from different social and cultural contexts fail to understand each other properly. People from different cultures have some points in common 1._____ but many more differences. Some of the differences can be seen in expectations when visiting someone. For example, 2._____ and how time is used in a culture reveal how members of that culture 3._____ time. Cultures 4._____ in the notion of time and the way to efficiently use it. Monochronic time (M-time) culture, the culture characteristic of Western countries, places great emphasis on 5._____. Visitors who "drop by" without 6._____ may interrupt the host's personal time and be considered impolite. In contrast, Polychronic time (P-time) culture emphasizes 7._____, and rigidly adheres to the clock. Therefore, in the M-culture of Western countries, if you are going to visit someone, you should 8._____ in advance, giving others enough time to make arrangements. In answering an invitation, Western people would let the host know whether he/she would accept it or not as soon as possible, while people from P-time culture are 9._____ and more flexible. When visiting someone's home, consideration of the host's time value can 10._____ a pleasant visit both for yourself and for your hosts.

SECTION 2 CHECK YOUR MANNERS

Read the following statements, then mark T for the true statements and F for the false statements. Provide corrections for the false ones.

___ 1. Ask who else is coming when you are invited to an event.

___ 2. Accept the invitation even though you are not sure whether you really plan to go.

___ 3. Bringing an uninvited guest to an event is considered rude since in some cases it's a question of annoyance or social embarrassment; in others it's a matter of considerable additional expense.

___ 4. Guest responsibilities include dressing appropriately for the occasion and providing one's own transportation and lodging.

___ 5. When receiving an invitation, one is not obliged to respond as soon as possible.

___ 6. A good guest offers to help and insists if the offer is firmly refused.

___ 7. When you are invited for dinner, it is rude to call at the last minute for directions; but it's acceptable if you arrive early.

___ 8. When you have a pet, it is always proper to ask before you take it to someone else's home.

___ 9. When you accept an invitation, you are expected to show up; if you are unable to attend, call the host/hostess anytime before the social gathering.

___ 10. Never leave a party without saying good-bye, and follow up within 3 days with a thank-you card or a personal call to the host.

SECTION 3 PRACTICE

In this section, proper etiquette will be learned through different tasks.

Task 1 Matching the ways of greetings

Work in pairs to practice different ways of greeting in different parts of the world and match the appropriate behavior to its corresponding country in the table below.

1. Handshakes are used in business and social settings. It's important to make eye contact during a handshake.	A. Greece
2. People greet each other by touching the nose, foreheads, or both. When greeting, people press their foreheads and noses together and look into each other's eyes.	B. North America
3. A formal way to greet each other is to pat the other's shoulder or back.	C. France
4. When two people greet each other, they touch cheeks and kiss the air.	D. New Zealand

Task 2 Giving the gift

Answer the following questions and test what you know about gift-giving etiquette, and then role-play the scenario where you present the gift to the host or hostess.

1. Which is the appropriate response when the host receives a gift from the guests?

   A. I already have one.   B. How thoughtful.
   C. I'd like to return/exchange it for something else. D. It's not really my taste.
   E. Thank you.   F. Do you have the receipt?
   G. Does it come in a different color?   H. I know someone who could use this.
   I. I like it because it's from you.

2. What are unappreciated gifts when visiting a friend?

   A. Attractively wrapped kitchen tools   B. Flowers
   C. A special food from your country   D. A bottle of wine

E. Candy
F. A set of your country's coins
G. Inexpensive handicraft or a piece of art
H. A bunch of red roses
I. A bottle of Whisky
J. A selection of mint stamps from your country
K. A book about your country

Task 3 Making decisions on who has been invited

Discuss with your partners and decide who will attend the gathering if you have received the invitation addressed in the following ways.

1. Ms. Mary Smith
2. Mr. and Mrs. Jones
3. Ms. Mary Smith and Guest
4. Mr. and Mrs. Sam Jones and Family

Task 4 Using proper etiquette when visiting friends

Complete the conversation with the words or expressions given in the box in their proper forms, then role-play the conversation with a partner.

let your hosts know	watch the program they like	what they like
food allergies	invite me	thank-you note
visiting etiquette	unless	proper	taste and hobbies

Conversation

(*Martin is working in an international company. It is Friday. Martin is chatting with his colleague Amy.*)

Amy: Martin, do you have any plans for the weekend?

Martin: My boss and his wife 1._____ to visit their home this weekend. To be frank, I am a little nervous.

Amy: What are you nervous about?

Martin: I'm afraid I would break the etiquette rules. Please tell me something about 2._____ in Western countries.

Amy: Do you have a gift for your hosts?

Martin: Gift? But I have no idea about what is 3._____.

Amy: Here's what I do. I take a gift with me when I know my hosts' 4._____.

Martin: But I don't know their taste and hobbies.

Amy: When I don't have a clue, I pay attention to 5._____ while I am there. Then I send a special gift after the visit.

Martin: I'm afraid I am not used to the food they prepare. So, I plan to take some food with me.

Amy: Unless you have 6._____ or need to follow a special diet that would be rude. The rule is to "make do."

Martin: I don't have any food allergies. But what should I do if I don't like the food they prepare?

Amy: If there is something you don't like, don't 7._____. Have a little bit of everything to be polite but fill up on the things you like.

Martin: Yes, I will have a bit of everything and have more of the things I like. Trust me. I will not let the hosts know I don't like the food. And Amy, can I take my dog Freckles?

Amy: No way. 8._____ they invite Freckles. Ask your neighbors if they could look after him.

Martin: Can I watch TV there?

Amy: They may ask if you want to watch television and if you have any favorite shows. However, if you are not asked, you will 9._____.

Martin: Amy, is there anything else I should know?

Amy: Don't forget to send a handwritten 10._____ afterwards.

Martin: Is it necessary to send a handwritten one? Is it OK if I write an e-mail to thank the hosts?

Amy: No way. E-mail is too impersonal. Anyway, enjoy yourself.

Thank-you note

Complete the thank-you note with the words or expressions necessary for the occasion given in the box, and then write a thank-you note to your friend to express your gratefulness for his/her family hosting your family at their house the past weekend.

---

hosting our family at your house this past weekend   Mr. and Mrs.

see you once again   a special day   was so nice of you

Dear 11._____ Smith,

Thank you so much for 12._____. It was wonderful to 13._____. It brought back so many good memories to me.

It 14._____ to invite our family to your home. It was 15._____ and you are a special friend. Keep in touch!

Warmest wishes.

Sincerely,

…

SECTION 4   CASE STUDY

Read the following case which includes three short stories and do the case study in small groups. The questions in "Critical thinking" after the case are aimed to help with finding the story background, the problem itself, the etiquette involved, and the cultural differences behind the etiquette. Remember to provide possible solutions to the problem in the case.

Business with Displeasure

I threw a dinner party when I moved into my new place. I invited a few friends and told them to bring their significant others. My best friend had just started dating this new guy who was a hot-shot business type. He seemed a bit smarmy, but I figured I could deal with him. Once we sat down to eat, though, I knew I hated him. He put on his cell-phone headset and started taking calls at the table. He actually shushed the rest of us at one point because he was "talking to a client." Finally, I pulled my friend aside and got her to step in, but the whole mood of the dinner had already been ruined.

Up in Flames

My sister threw a great Halloween party last year. Everyone dressed up, she had put up decorations everywhere, and the food was great. The only problem was that she invited a college friend of hers who is totally immature. He always had to be the center of attention and would do anything to get it. He came dressed as a magician and whenever he wasn't getting enough attention, he would command that the entire party come to a halt so that everyone could watch him do a trick. His last trick involved waving a candle around and making things disappear. Well, he started waving it and as he was doing so, somehow my sister's curtains caught on fire. He didn't even notice at first and kept going. It wasn't until my sister started screaming that he realized what he had done. We threw water on it, but the party was pretty much done after that.

Self-Centered

A friend of mine with a history of being rather self-centered was invited with her partner to my daughter's first birthday barbecue. Not only did she park on our shared driveway (whereas the other 30 guests realized it would be better to park on the street so as not to block the neighbors, including my elderly and not very mobile relatives), but she turned up with a bottle of wine and two wine glasses. She and her partner uncorked the bottle and shared the whole thing between themselves. Not only did they not offer any to anyone else, but also to bring their own fancy glasses so they wouldn't have to drink out of a plastic cup seemed pretty snobby! I found the bottle of wine in the kitchen afterwards and commented to my husband that at least they left the rest here for us. But the bottle was empty and they hadn't bothered to put it in the recycle bin on their short walk to the most selfish parking possible.

Critical thinking

1. Retell the stories in the case in 3–4 sentences using the expressions in the box.

Business with Displeasure	dinner party bring significant others new guy take call mood ruined
Up in Flames	Halloween party college friend immature be the center of attention wave a candle caught on fire party pretty much done
Self-Centered	friend self-centered park on the shared driveway share the whole bottle of wine not bother to put the empty bottle in the recycle bin

2. Why were the guests unpopular in the stories?

3. What do the stories suggest about proper visiting etiquette when one is being a guest at a party or someone's home?

SECTION 5   READING FOR ETIQUETTE TIPS

Read the following passages and finish the exercises after each of the texts.

Passage 1

Guest Etiquette in Western Culture

The good guest is almost invisible, enjoying him or herself, communing with fellow guests, and, most of all, enjoying the generous hospitality of the hosts.

— Emily Post

The guest-host relationship is not one-sided: hosts doing all the work and guests just showing up. Socializing should be a two-sided activity where hosts see to the comfort of the guests and the guests respond with their company and respect.

Some people receive piles of invitations; others, few or none. Being the perfect guest, the one people love to have over for all occasions from intimate family gatherings to major social events, means following some basic rules. Etiquette is not some outdated code. Manners are not an old-fashioned snobbish affectation but a good roadmap to courteous behavior.

Don't ask who else is coming

Don't ask who else is coming when you are invited. Such an inquiry implies that the invitation is not attractive unless certain notable people will be present.

Ascertain your presence

Don't leave your host in suspense about your attendance at the party (unless you are planning a fun surprise). If the hosts have asked for confirmation, inform them in time, whether your answer is positive or negative. It will help them in their preparations.

Never bring an uninvited guest

Do not bring a friend along without first asking the hostess. If she says you may, introduce whoever it is to the host and hostess when you arrive.

— Nancy Tuckerman and Nancy Duncan

If you receive an invitation that says bringing additional guests is fine, go for it. If your invitation does not specify whether you can bring your own guests, go by this rule: For a formal event such as a wedding, do not bring guests; for an informal event such as a birthday party or a cookout, ask the host first.

Be on time

Another attribute of the perfect guest is never to keep people waiting.

— Emily Post

When invited for dinner, be punctual, making allowances for traffic jams or finding a parking space. Arriving too early or calling at the last minute for directions will make the host or hostess awkward when they are dashing around seeing to a hundred and one last-minute details. Being ten to fifteen minutes late is acceptable, but any later than that shows a lack of consideration. Above all, never cancel at the last minute, except in a **dire** (可怕的) emergency.

Bring a gift to your host/hostess

Whether you are carrying a small **duffle bag** (帆布袋) or a designer handbag, make sure a gift for your hosts is packed. Something from your home is recommended and shows **forethought** (事先考虑). If the hosts have children, it is a nice touch to bring something for them. Thoughtful little gifts are always appreciated.

- Flowers are considered by most to be a very thoughtful gift for most occasions, such as birthdays and weddings. But there are some taboos when taking flowers as a gift: first, red roses signify a romantic interest; second, an even number of flowers signifies bad luck, as does the number thirteen; and third, always unwrap the flowers before presenting them.

- A beautiful box of chocolates or **gourmet** (美食家) products like a fine olive oil, **balsamic vinegar** (香醋), spices or **condiments** (调味品) are always appreciated.

- In addition, a best-selling book, CD or video are proper gifts presented to the host/hostess.

- A decorative picture frame, photo album or photo box are ideal for the host to store holiday season memories.

No pets, please

Perhaps the greatest damage that most of us are ever asked to bear is that caused by a lap dog which is taken everywhere and allowed to run free.

—Emily Post

Unless your host has made it clear that this would be the perfect time for a doggie play-date, you can manage to tear yourself away from dear dog for a little while. Other guests may be reluctant to become caked in dog **slobber** (口水), or are deadly **allergic** (过敏) to the kitten in your pocket, or they may harbor a secret **phobia** (恐惧症) of iguanas. Even if everyone at the event adores the animal you have brought, it makes it hard to socialize when you're constantly getting up to **wrangle** (争吵), discipline, or otherwise tend to the pet.

Be a thoughtful guest

If you notice your hostess is busy, ask if she'd like you to help remove the dirty plates.

—Nancy Tuckerman and Nancy Duncan

Offering to help is great, but if the host says "no thanks," stay out of their way, especially if it is in the kitchen. Do always offer some help at the end of a meal. An offer to assist with the collection of glasses, or just any help makes you a good guest, but be sure you have permission to do so.

Rules for smokers

Don't smoke in the home of non-smokers (their numbers are growing). Never light up during the meal; it would spoil the food and wine being served. If possible, forgo smoking after dinner or ask permission. And respect the unspoken wishes behind a reluctant "yes."

When it's time to go, go

Don't overstay your welcome; if an ending time was given on the invitation, leave shortly after the time indicated.

— Nancy Tuckerman and Nancy Duncan

Don't leave too early; it often breaks up the party—your hostess wants you to stay a while and have a good time. But if your hostess is wearily putting away the last of the leftovers, slowly wiping down tables, or excusing herself to get into her pajamas, you should have gone an hour ago. And after you say you need to go, get up, say goodbye, and leave. You are not required to stand in the doorway for another half-hour talking to the hostess just to assure her that you enjoyed her event. Thank your host and hostess warmly but don't dally in the hall or at the door.

Reciprocate (酬答)

It is true that a return invitation should, when possible, be paid for every first invitation.

—Emily Post

Are you always a guest and never a host? Accepting the invitations of others and never tendering your own makes it seem like you don't enjoy their company, but feel obligated to attend their events for some reason.

Thank–you note

When you arrive home, write a thank-you note within 3 days, or no later than 1 week and, perhaps, to tell your host family that you appreciate their hospitality or offer to be a host in the future. The considerable house guest leaves the hosts wanting to see you more often. After all, one invitation leads to another!

Exercises

Choose the best answer to each question.

1. A two-sided activity means _____.

    A. hosts do all the preparation work in advance and guests just show up to have fun

    B. hosts and guests exchange gifts and cards

    C. hosts see to the guests' comfort and guests respond with company and respect

    D. guests promise to host a return invitation

2. Which of the following statements is TRUE?

    A. Manners are an old-fashioned affection.

B. Manners are a good roadmap to courteous behavior.

C. Etiquette is an outdated code of behavior.

D. Etiquette means receiving piles of invitations.

3. Good manners include the following EXCEPT _____.

   A. ascertaining your presence whether your answer is positive or negative

   B. never bringing an uninvited guest to a formal event

   C. always offering help at the end of the meal

   D. calling at the last minute if you cannot be present

4. It is proper time to go _____.

   A. any moment during the event

   B. immediately after the event begins

   C. an hour before your hostess slowly wipes down tables

   D. when your hostess excuses herself to get into her pajamas

5. Write a thank-you note _____.

   A. the very day you took part in the event

   B. to express your appreciation of the hosts' hospitality

   C. any time after you took part in the event

   D. to offer to be the guest again in the future

Passage 2

Thank-You Note

Write a stand-out thank-you note to a hostess or gift-giver with our tips for a thoughtful, sincere message.

— By Jennifer Beeler

Many people underestimate the power of the hand-written thank-you note. Some think it is better to send an immediate email or simply say thanks in person. But a hand-written note is the ideal way to show your appreciation. With the ever-growing popularity of technology, the art of writing an "old-school" note is being lost. It may seem **daunting** (令人望而却步的) and maybe a bit **archaic** (过时的) to pick up a pen and a stationery card, but just remember these tips and you'll soon be a pro.

Do's

• Handwrite the thank-you note. Don't just apply these tips to your email thank-yous. Although it would be easier to send an email or type a letter, a handwritten thank-you note is the most sincere and appreciated form of gratitude. The extra effort goes a long way.

• Buy stationery. **Embossed** (饰以浮饰的) cards with complementary envelopes look much better than folded notebook paper stuffed into a plain envelope. You don't have to **splurge** (挥霍) on embossed or **monogrammed** (雕花的) stationery from a specialty store. You can find decent sets at office supply stores and online.

• Personalize it. Not just in the personalized stationery, but in what you actually say. If you're going to see the person in the future, refer to the event and say you're looking forward to it. If the person gave you a silver picture frame, don't simply thank them for it, but add, "I plan on using the frame for a wedding picture in my living room."

• Even if it's late, send a note. Don't feel embarrassed. It's better to send a late thank-you than none at all.

• Take your time. An illegible note won't do much good and neither will one with scratch marks all over it. Use a nice, fine point pen, so the ink won't bleed or **smudge** (涂污). Traditionally, thank-you notes are written in **cursive** (草写体) writing. Sometimes this can look like a mess if your cursive writing is not **up-to-par** (合乎标准), so use your best judgment and do what you think looks best.

• Send thanks for trivial things. Why not? Whether it's for a casual get-together or for a neighbor who collected your mail and watered your plants while you were gone, a hand-written note is the best way to show your appreciation. It may also ensure that you'll get the invitation or extra help in the future.

Don'ts
• Don't exaggerate. Of course, you can **rave about** (盛赞) a gift, but don't lie about how much you like something. It may be obvious if you say, "The monogrammed soap is the most beautiful thing I have ever seen!" Most likely you've seen better, so simply say, "The monogrammed soap was very thoughtful and will be perfect for the powder room."

• Don't be stiff. Show your personality. It's okay to use humor, sarcasm, or idioms to express yourself, as long as you're not insulting the gift. If you're questioning whether you should write a certain joke or phrase, ask yourself if you would say it in-person. Try to maintain the same tone with the person on paper as you would in-person.

• Don't refer to specific amounts of money. These might seem like the hardest notes to write, but all you have to say is "I greatly appreciate your generosity. I hope to use the money to …" Just make sure the giver would support your money plans. Your great-aunt may not support a weekend getaway to Vegas, but she would understand a "much-needed vacation."

• Don't **ramble** (长篇大论). You may want to go on and on about how your new job is going, a family friend you ran into, or that new movie you saw, but don't. Be concise. It is a thank-you note after all, so stick to the thanks. If you feel like writing more, write them a separate note to fill them in on your life and see how they're doing.

• Don't assume an in-person thanks is enough. If a person went to the trouble of hosting a party or purchasing a gift for you, you surely can take the time to write a note. Make sure to thank the host of a party in-person, but since your thanks may get lost in the excitement, a note is a great addition.

Exercises
Choose the best answer to each question.

1. It is an ideal way to show your appreciation by _____.
    A. sending an immediate email
    B. writing a hand-written thank-you note
    C. sending a carefully selected gift
    D. saying thanks in person
2. Which of the following statements demonstrates "Personalize it"?
    A. Buy monogrammed stationary from a specialty store.
    B. Tell the person you're looking forward to an event where you two are going to meet.
    C. Just use the gift item and don't mention it in a thank-you note.
    D. Say whatever you want to say to the gift-giver.
3. A good thank-you note includes the following EXCEPT _____.
    A. finding decent sets of stationery at office supply stores and online
    B. sending a note even though it's late
    C. sending an email if your handwriting is not up-to-par
    D. expressing your appreciation even for trivial things
4. "Don't be stiff" refers to _____.
    A. don't be sarcastic on paper
    B. don't insult the gift
    C. write a certain joke or phrase on paper which you would not say in-person
    D. maintain the same tone with the person on paper as you would in-person
5. Which of the following does not make a good thank-you note?
    A. Writing as much as possible ranging from your new job to the new movie you saw.

B. Taking the time to write a note even though you made an in-person thanks.

C. Not mentioning specific amount of money to the giver.

D. Not telling lies to say that the gift is the best one you've ever seen.

SECTION 6   CULTURAL EXPLORATION

In this section, you will learn Chinese etiquette from the cultural perspective.

Task 1   Understanding Chinese etiquette in ancient poems or famous quotes

Read and study the following ancient Chinese poem related to visiting a friend in English and then find out its original Chinese version. What message is being conveyed in this poem?

Visiting an Old Friend's Cottage

By Meng Haoran

Translated by Xu Yuanchong

My friend's prepared chicken and rice;

I'm invited to his cottage hall.

Green trees surround the village nice;

Blue hills slant beyond the city wall.

Windows open to field and ground;

Over wine we talk of crops of grain.

On Double Ninth Day I'll come around;

For the chrysanthemums again.

_____

作者_____

译者_____

_____
_____
_____
_____
_____
_____

Task 2 Learning Chinese traditions related to the etiquette of this unit

Read the following introduction to the Chinese drinking culture and identify the major cultural points included in this passage. Then pick out some key words or cultural expressions that help you remember and understand the major points.

> In China, stories of drinking liquor can be traced back to almost every period of Chinese history. Many customs concerning alcohol have formed and evolved over the years which had and have become part of Chinese daily life.
>
> Alcohol is part of Chinese folklore, and is intricately linked with social interaction. In modern China, alcohol appears in almost all social activities, ranging from birthday parties for seniors, wedding feasts, to dinner at a friend's home. On all the occasions liquor is the main drink to show respect or happiness. Drinking provides more opportunities for one to make more friends as the old saying goes, "Frequent drinking makes friends surrounding." Moreover, alcohol also serves effectively to deepen and strengthen friendships. Since it shows one's friendliness, alcohol is always used to relieve misunderstanding and hatred no matter how strong it is. "A thousand cups of wine is not too much when bosom friends meet," according to an old Chinese saying. In fact, drinking together is an essential part of socializing. Alcohol is generally a welcome gift when one visits Chinese friends on special occasions. It is a simple gift that can come in a variety of options. Upon visiting a friend, one can not go wrong with a nice bottle of white liquor (Baijiu) or a bottle of wine. However, with many people laying great emphasis on health in modern society, drinking in moderation has become widely accepted.
>
> It is said that alcohol had a greater impact on Chinese artists than any other social group, since many of them had produced their peak-of-perfection masterpieces right after drinking. Being drunk and in a state of free production is an important tip Chinese artists resort to to free their artistic creativity. Many famous poets, such as Li Bai and Du Fu, produced surprisingly marvelous poems after drinking the mysterious liquid. Not only poems but also paintings and calligraphy were raised to a higher level by the aid of drinking alcohol. Wang Xizhi, a Chinese famous calligrapher respectfully called the Calligraphy Saint, retried dozens of times to outdo his most outstanding work, "Lantingji Xu" (Orchid Pavilion Prologue) which he finished when he was drunk, but he failed. The original one was the best.

1. Major cultural points in the story:

    (1) _____

    (2) _____

(3) _____

2. Major words or cultural expressions in the story:

   (1) Para. 1 _____

   (2) Para. 2 _____

   (3) Para. 3 _____

3. What interesting stories about alcohol-drinking in ancient China would you like to share with your classmates?

Unit 2
Hosting the Home Guests

You will learn in this unit
- ☐ invitation etiquette
- ☐ house hosting etiquette
- ☐ dealing with uninvited guests
- ☐ cultural gap between East and West on hosting an event

SECTION 1 INTRODUCTION

🔊 Listen to the following passage and fill in the blanks.

Hosting guests is an art, which requires 1._____ about etiquette, being considerate and well-rounded. People from East and West are all very careful about their hosting etiquette. When friends are arriving, 2._____, both in the East and the West, would 3._____ in regard to hosting issues like house cleaning, venue setting as well as the provision of food and drinks. However, countries from 4._____ have formed various hosting customs along with their 5._____. Lack of knowledge of cultural features of a country would bring about misunderstandings between people of 6._____. For example, shaking hands is the most common 7._____ etiquette in east Asian countries, while Western people 8._____ when people meet each other or say goodbye. Also, when hosting guests, people from different cultures would 9._____ in different ways. Western people may prefer saying "help yourself" instead of insisting helping the guest personally. 10._____ in different cultures would be of great help when hosting a foreign friend.

SECTION 2 CHECK YOUR MANNERS

Read the following statements, then mark T for the true statements and F for the false statements. Provide corrections for the false ones.

___ 1. If you're a doctor or a dietician, it's your job as a host or hostess to monitor the calorie, fat, cholesterol, or curb the food intake of your guests or give advice about weight loss or gain.

___ 2. As the host/hostess, do make sure no guest dominates the conversation at the expense of other guests.

___ 3. While it is gracious of guests to offer to bring things, don't expect them to offer.

___ 4. The host or hostess doesn't have to find out if any guests have food allergies or special diets since the guests are adults and they are capable of looking after themselves.

___ 5. As the host, you are bringing these people together. It is not your job to help them interact. They will find the topic and the person they are interested in to interact with.

___ 6. When you are having a party at your home, greet guests at the door, and make the effort to smile.

___ 7. Current party etiquette allows for as much as possible early arrival for guests, so be prepared.

__ 8. For guests who don't seem to want to leave, there are some indirect methods to give them the hint. Start to wind down the gathering by offering coffee, blowing out candles and turning off the music. Offer to package up leftover food for them to take home and gather their coats and other belongings.

__ 9. If you've served alcohol at the gathering, you must take some responsibility as to the health and safety of any drinkers.

__ 10. Find out what kind of food they like and whether there are any special dietary restrictions or if they have any allergies before the arrival of the guests.

SECTION 3 PRACTICE

In this section, proper etiquette will be learned through different tasks.

Task 1 Choosing proper time to invite

Whether you're mailing invitations or inviting guests by phone, timing is key. Send an invitation too late and the guest may already be booked; send it too early and it might be misplaced or forgotten. Discuss with your partners and decide when to invite your guests on each of the following occasions.

Event	When to Invite
Anniversary party	3 to 6 weeks before the event
Casual party	
Christmas party	
Cocktail party	
Formal dinner	
Graduation party	
Housewarming party	
Informal dinner	
Lunch or Tea	
Thanksgiving dinner	

Task 2 Meeting unexpected guests

A carefully planned party can fall apart when an unexpected guest shows up, while it's extremely rude for an invited guest to bring a friend without first checking with the host. Choose what a host or hostess should do when there is an unexpected guest from the items in Table 1 to complete Table 2 (some of the answers have been given), and then role-play it with your partners.

Table 1

No.	Items
A	Kick into full host mode and make them feel welcome.
B	It is appropriate to say no when there might be awkwardness between them and one of your guests. For example, bringing ex-spouses, ex-boyfriends, ex-girlfriends or those who have suffered a serious falling out could create a difficult situation.
C	When the invited guests respond to your RSVP, give them the details of the event.
D	After the party, make sure you politely and privately confront the offender who brought the uninvited guest.
E	State that while you enjoyed getting to know so-and-so, you found it incredibly stressful to have to accommodate an extra person with no notice.
F	Say that you're looking forward to getting together.
G	Set another place at the table.
H	If an invited guest mentions that they'd like to bring someone when they RSVP, decide how to respond.
I	If someone brings several other people to your party, you are within your rights to say that you simply cannot accommodate them.
J	Pleasantly joke with them that they'd better not surprise you with uninvited guests.
K	Do what you can to include the unexpected guest in the conversations since they will likely not know anyone at the party.

Table 2

Handle the situation before the party	1	
	2	
	3	J
	4	
Deal with the problem at a party	5	A
	6	
Make room to smooth over an awkward lack of notice	7	G

Unit 2 Hosting the Home Guests

		Continued
When to say no	8	
	9	
Confront the offender	10	
	11	

Task 3 Behaving well in different occasions

Complete the conversations with the words or expressions necessary for each occasion with the help of the word bank, and then role-play them with a partner.

> is driving   be off   won a prize
> how nice to see you   not yet surely   for coming
> delighted to see   very kind of you   thank you very much

Conversation 1

Amy: If you'll excuse me, I really should 1._____ now.
Bob: 2._____. Have another drink at least.
Amy: No, thank you all the same.
Bob: Oh dear! What a pity!
Amy: 3._____ indeed for the delicious meal.
Bob: Thank you 4._____.

Conversation 2

Mrs. Phillips: 5._____, Mrs. Adams. Do come in. I'll take your coat. Henry … Henry … Mr. and Mrs. Adams are here.
Mrs. Adams: It's 6._____ to invite us. Is it a special occasion?
Mr. Phillips: Good evening, Mrs. Adams. Good evening, sir. What would you like to drink?
Mr. Adams: My wife 7._____ tonight so I'll need something strong.
Mr. Phillips: Follow me. Everyone's in the sitting room.

(*In the sitting room.*)

Mr. Phillips: Ladies and gentlemen, I'd like to tell you the reason for this party. Of course, we're always 8._____ all of you but … what I want to say is … Helen has just 9._____. She entered a competition and we're going to Bermuda on a free holiday.

SECTION 4 CASE STUDY

Read the following cases and do each case study in small groups. The questions in "Critical thinking" after each case are aimed to help with finding the story background, the problem itself, the etiquette involved, and the cultural differences behind the etiquette. Remember to provide possible solutions to the problem in each case.

Case 1

Understanding Chinese Modesty

Why is it that when you study a foreign language, you never learn the little phrases that let you slip into a culture without all your foreignness exposed? Every Chinese-language textbook starts out with the standard phrase for greeting people; but as an American, I constantly found myself tongue-tied when it came to seeing guests off at the door. An abrupt goodbye would not do, yet that was all I had ever learned from these books. So I would smile and nod, bowing and trying to find words that would smooth over the visitors' leaving and make them feel they would be welcome to come again. In my **fluster** (慌乱), I often hid behind my Chinese husband's **graciousness** (谦和).

Then finally, listening to others, I began to pick up the phrases that eased relations and sent people off with a feeling of mission not only accomplished but **surpassed** (超越).

Partings for the Chinese involve a certain amount of ritual and a great deal of **one-upmanship** (胜人一筹). Although I'm not expected to observe or even know all the rules, as a foreigner, I've had to learn the expressions of politeness and protest that accompany a farewell.

The Chinese feel they must see a guest off to the farthest feasible point down a flight of stairs to the street below or perhaps all the way to the nearest bus stop. I've sometimes waited half an hour or more for my husband to return from seeing a guest off, since he's gone to the bus stop and waited for the next bus to arrive.

For a less important or perhaps a younger guest, he may simply say, "I won't see you off, all right?" And of course the guest assures him that he would never think of putting him to the trouble of seeing him off. "Don't see me off! Don't see me off!"

American and Chinese cultures are at polar opposites. An American hostess, complimented for her cooking skills, is likely to say, "Oh, I'm so glad that you liked it. I cooked it especially for you." Not so a Chinese host or hostess, who will instead apologize for giving you "nothing" even slightly edible and for not showing you enough honor by providing proper dishes.

The Chinese take pride in "modesty"; the Americans in "straightforwardness." That modesty has left many a Chinese hungry at an American table, for Chinese politeness calls for three refusals before one accepts an offer, and the American hosts take a "no" to mean "no," whether it's the first, second, or third time.

Once you've learned the signals and how to respond, life becomes much easier. When guests come, I know I should immediately ask if they'd like a cup of tea. They will respond, "Please don't bother," which is my signal to fetch tea.

Critical thinking

1. Retell the case in 3–4 sentences using the expressions in the box.

without foreignness exposed	pick up the phrases
see off	compliment
modesty	straightforwardness

2. What cultural differences between China and America can you draw from the text?

3. How different is Chinese hospitality from that in Western culture when hosting friends in different situations, like mentioned in this case? Please give more examples.

Case 2

A Surprising Dinner

Not too long after moving to London, my friend and I were invited over to dinner by a local couple. We gratefully accepted and politely insisted that they don't go to too much trouble for us. On the night of the dinner, we stopped off and bought two nice bottles of wine as I believe it is impolite to show up empty-handed.

As we finished off helping with the dinner dishes, the couple then turned to us and told us exactly that our share of the cost of the ingredients for dinner is split down to the last penny. Frankly, my understanding is if you invite someone over for a meal, unless it is a "bring your own plate" event then it goes without saying that you are prepared to buy all the ingredients yourself. The guests then do their part by bringing either wine or a small gift (chocolates or flowers etc.) to show their appreciation for the effort the hosts had gone to.

We were also planning to reciprocate the dinner invitation. However, we changed our minds after the grocery receipt was presented to us. Stunned, we paid up, thinking maybe this was a new custom or some modern rule of etiquette we had failed to become aware of.

Critical thinking

1. Retell the case in 3–4 sentences using the expressions in the box.

gratefully accepted	empty-handed	our share of the cost
stunned	failed to	

2. Why did the author and her friend change their minds of inviting the couple to dinner after the grocery receipt was presented to them?

3. List hosting etiquette in Chinese culture and discuss in groups the merits which should be inherited and the customs which may bring about problems in intercultural communication.

SECTION 5 READING FOR ETIQUETTE TIPS

Read the following passages and finish the exercises after each of the texts.

Passage 1

Being a Courteous Host

A host's job is to ensure that everyone is comfortable and has a good time. Hosts and guests alike have responsibilities. Being a good guest **entails** (需要) more than just showing up with a bottle of wine or a bunch of flowers to a dinner party. Similarly, hosts need to consider that there is a lot more to plan an event.

The invitation

• Invite the guests. Send out invitations for the party if you have a huge crowd. Otherwise, you can call everyone personally and inform them, and a face-to-face invitation works even better if you're just inviting over a couple of friends.

• Provide as much information as possible to guests ahead of time. Whichever method you choose, make sure you update them with all the information about the social gathering. Make the rules clear about having extra guests at this point. If you are open to this, prepare to receive them as well with extra food and drinks.

The preparation

• Clean your house. Keep the house clean before guests arrive. Your house will probably be messy after the party anyway, but making a good first impression is vital to making sure that people not only come back to your house in the future, but also that you have a good reputation.

• Prepare for special diets. Find out if anyone is a vegetarian or has some kind of allergy. Keep alcoholic as well as non-alcoholic drinks to avoid disappointing anyone.

• Always have something to eat and drink. Assess the number of guests you'll be entertaining. Every event will require you to offer food and drink, ranging from snacks and sodas to a five-course meal. Keep in mind food allergies that people may have. If you're just getting together for a few minutes, have tea, coffee, juice, soda, and some snacks. For mornings, have brunch foods. For afternoons and evenings, have desserts and **savory** (可口的；咸味的) snacks. If you're planning a party, a gathering that will last more than a few hours, or a gathering that happens during a typical meal time, always have a meal planned.

• Have emergency medical supplies that are easily accessible. Keep first-aid and cleaning items ready so that you can attend to any injuries or spills immediately. This is especially needed if there are children in the gathering.

The arrival

• Express your appreciation when receiving a gift. Always put a smile on your face as a gift is being presented. Receive the gift with both hands. Say thank you along with a brief expression of appreciation.

• Be sensitive to opening a gift in front of others. Americans typically open gifts as soon as it is received, even in front of an audience and other groups of people. However, in many countries it is not customary or appropriate to open gifts in front of other people. They are kept to be opened when alone. When receiving house gifts from special guests, be sensitive as to whether you will or will not be encouraged and expected to open it right away.

• Greet each guest cheerfully. Greet both adults and children cheerfully. Don't just say hi to the entire group. Address each person individually, and give guests a brief tour, so they can find important rooms, like bathrooms, by themselves.

• Make your house rules known. Since everyone has a different idea of appropriate party behavior, let guests know about any rules you have. For example, if you have a rule about not bringing food into a certain room, you need to tell your guests about it or post a sign about it in a prominent location.

- Don't keep your guests waiting. If you are serving dinner, serve it at the appointed hour even if someone hasn't shown up yet. A late guest will expect to have missed some of the food and fun, and shouldn't be rewarded for being late by **garnering** (获得) special consideration. Don't spend the first hour of your party fixing and re-fixing your hair in your bedroom, while your guests **mill about** (大群人无目的地乱转) awkwardly.

Fifteen minutes is the established length of time that a hostess may wait for a belated guest. To wait more than twenty minutes, at the outside, would be showing lack of consideration to many for the sake of one.

—Emily Post

- Relax and have a good time. If your guests can see that you're enjoying yourself, they'll be more likely to have a good time too. If you seem stressed out or disappointed in how the party's going, your attitude will carry over into how your guests see the party. Do not call attention to anything that goes wrong, whether it be your own fault or someone else's.

The best hosts are relaxed and welcoming, not worried about getting things right.

—Sarah Neish

Those who love to give parties usually give them with ease, which means an unworried attitude of mind. Even if a dozen things go wrong, they know that few of their friends will notice, and fewer still will care, and after all why should things go wrong?

—Emily Post

- Steer the conversation away from uncomfortable topics. A good religious or political discussion can be stimulating in the context of friends enjoying an evening together, but such topics should be avoided among mere acquaintances who have widely differing opinions. Also, the host should steer the conversation away from overly personal topics and be prepared to change the subject deliberately if an **inadvertent** (无意中做的) remark causes offense. A good host does not allow one of his guests to be made to feel uncomfortable by another guest.

- It's not over until it's over. Although you may have **envisioned** (预想) yourself finished with cleaning and sitting on the couch sipping tea by 10:00 p.m., if your guests decide to stay until 2:00 a.m. you must do your best to keep going. No matter how tired you are, do not let the guests feel that you are anxious for them to leave.

If you expect your guests to enjoy themselves, don't make them feel as though they have overstayed their welcome, even if they have.

—Sarah Neish

The departure

● Remind **lingering** (逗留) guests. For guests who don't seem to want to leave, there are some indirect methods to give them the hint. Start to wind down the party by offering coffee, blowing out candles and turning off the music. Offer to package up leftover food for them to take home and gather their coats and other belongings. If they still don't get it, a more direct approach is needed. Simply and politely state your request, such as, "Thank you for coming, but it's getting late and I have a lot to do. Let me walk you to your car."

● Farewell to guests. As the party winds down, your host duties gear up again, especially regarding cocktail party etiquette. If you've served alcohol at the party, you must take some responsibility as to the health and safety of any drinkers. If you notice that someone has been drinking excessively, it's entirely your responsibility to call a cab or otherwise arrange a ride home for him or her. You may be held legally responsible for any injury or damage as a result of alcohol served at your party.

Finally, make sure to express your appreciation to your guests as you help them gather their things, and thank each guest for coming over and tell them how much you loved having them visit. If they brought any gifts, be sure to thank them for the gifts. It's a nice touch to reference a specific conversation you had with each guest as they leave. Walk guests to the door, and see that they make it safely into their vehicle. This way, guests feel cared for from the minute they arrive until the final farewells.

Exercises

Choose the best answer to each question.

1. According to the passage, if you invite a couple of friends, you should _____.
    A. send out a formal invitation
    B. call everyone personally and inform them
    C. invite them face-to-face
    D. ask a friend to tell them

2. What is the typical American way to open a gift from your guest?
    A. Open the gift alone as soon as it is received.
    B. Open the gift as soon as it is received in front of the guest.
    C. Open the gift in front of the guest when the party ends.
    D. Open the gift after the guest left.

3. Being a good host, you should let your guest see _____.
    A. you are enjoying yourself

B. you are caring about everyone

C. you are busy offering help

D. you are too stressed to help everyone

4. According to the passage, religious or political discussions should be avoided _____.

   A. in any circumstances

   B. when good friends are enjoying the evening together

   C. among unfamiliar people

   D. when the host announces the rules

5. What should the host do when it is time to farewell?

   A. Say thanks to those who have brought gifts.

   B. Walk the guests to the door.

   C. Ensure the safety of those who have drunk alcohol.

   D. All the above.

Passage 2

Understanding Cultural Differences in Hospitality

Sarah A. Lanier has lived and worked cross-culturally for many years and in her book *Foreign to Familiar* she **lumps**（大致区分）typical cultural traits into two categories: "hot culture" and "cold culture." Her generalizations are helpful in giving insight into relationships. This passage will cover a few of the main ideas of her book, with the intention of applying it in the context of cross-cultural hospitality.

What are hot and cold cultures?

Lanier categorizes everyone into either hot or cold culture categories. The main difference is that for hot (sometimes rural/tribal) cultures the ruling value is relationships, while for cold (sometimes urban) cultures, the ruling value is efficiency.

What are the key differences between people of hot cultures and people of cold cultures?

• Relationship orientation vs. task orientation. People from hot cultures tend to build their lives around people and relationships, while people from cold cultures tend to plan in terms of tasks and timelines.

• Indirect communication vs. direct communication. People from hot cultures tend to prefer indirect communication and don't want to harm a relationship by giving an answer someone does not want to hear. Cold cultures tend to prioritize direct communication because it "gets the job done"!

- Group Identity vs. individualism. Hot cultures raise children who see themselves as a part of a larger group (family, school, church, etc.). People from hot cultures will often maintain very close contact with their extended family, often living inter-generationally under the same roof throughout their adult lives. Cold cultures tend to think more individualistically—"I'll do it my way"—and raise their children to live on their own and make decisions more independently.

- Inclusion vs. privacy. Because of the group mentality of people from hot cultures, they automatically expect to be included or include others in whatever is happening in their presence. People from cold cultures tend to be more individualistic, meaning that they expect to be given a measure of privacy or to be asked if someone else can join the group.

Tips for people of cold cultures hosting people of hot cultures

If you're someone from a cold culture who's seeking to bridge gaps and make friendships with people from hot cultures, these ideas may help.

- Small talk is important in relationships with people from hot cultures. "Getting straight to business" is the cold-culture, task-oriented way of visiting with someone, but people from a hot culture prioritize a feel-good atmosphere.

- Your friend from a hot culture will be willing to flex his schedule or time for your relationship, and will likely expect the same in return.

- Good hospitality is best offered in your home, because a restaurant is impersonal. An overnight guest from a hot culture may feel hurt if you put him or her up in a hotel instead of at your home.

- Feel free to spontaneously drop in on your hot culture friend, but don't expect that he will necessarily drop everything he is doing when you arrive. He may just invite you along to do what he was already doing (going to pick up the kids, watering the garden or cooking supper) when you dropped in.

- Guests from hot cultures may value making you feel good more than telling you the truth. It might be difficult to tell when someone of a hot culture needs to say "no" but is saying "yes" because he or she wants to preserve your relationship. People from hot cultures will almost always say "yes" to a direct question because they feel rude saying "no." One way to overcome this and find out the truth about a situation may be to ask indirectly—go through another person to ask indirect questions around a topic that needs discussing.

- People from hot cultures often enjoy having someone with them at all times. Lanier wrote about being hosted in Africa, where the hostess purposely put another guest in the room "so you won't have to be alone." The loneliness of a hot culture person living in a cold culture can be overwhelming, because he or she is not used to living life and making so many decisions on his or her own. Being aware of this can help you to offer companionship or help in ways your hot culture friend really appreciates.

• A longer-term guest from a hot culture who is staying with you may assume he or she is included in anything that is going on, and may expect that everything will be shared or done together. Be careful—your guest may feel slighted if you mention something you'll be doing without intending to invite him or her along.

• Food in particular is seen as something to be shared. Taking food along to share with people of a hot culture builds relationships. In a hot culture, Lanier generalizes that "no one is left out, no one is lonely." Possessions are often shared in hot cultures; it's not "my" bike, it's "our" bike.

• People from hot cultures may appreciate being included, even spontaneously and even by a stranger. Lanier wrote about how she was eating alone at a restaurant, saw a Mexican family eating at a nearby table, and asked if she could eat with them. They thought it was completely normal to eat together and were in fact happy that she had asked to eat with them. Asking someone of a hot culture for a ride if they are going where you are going is almost expected—they would think it strange for you to go somewhere on your own, anyway!

• Usually in hot cultures, the host takes care of his overnight guest's expenses, and the guest brings a gift.

• Whole families are usually included in events outside of the workplace. People from hot cultures don't really understand "adults only" events in the same way people of cold cultures would. When you invite your hot culture contacts to spend time with you outside of working hours, know that they might assume they can bring their families along.

Tips for people of hot cultures hosting people of cold cultures
• Usually a friend from a cold culture feels respected when you honour his or her time by being punctual. Your friend probably thinks in terms of tasks to be completed that day, and may have other things on his or her schedule.

• Cold culture guests appreciate planning and advance invitations. Their refusal of an invitation may not be because they don't want to come—it may simply be because your last-minute invitation for Saturday lunch interfered with their efficient Saturday plans prepared days in advance.

• What your host or guest considers honest communication, you may consider too direct. Try not to take offence, and be grateful that your cold culture friend is telling you what he or she truly wants! If you ask a preference, you may not get the answer you hoped for, but you will usually find out the truth.

• If your cold culture guest is staying with you overnight or for an extended period, he or she may enjoy having some time alone. People of cold cultures generally appreciate privacy and/or a private room to sleep in when possible.

• People of cold cultures may or may not include family members in invitations to socialize outside the workplace. Be sure to indicate whether spouses and children are also invited to parties you are hosting.

• If you are staying with a cold culture host, be aware that in cold cultures, hospitality is often seen as something that takes the host's full attention, whether it is for an afternoon or for days at time. For this reason, asking to stay with a cold culture host for an extended period of time might sound overwhelming to him or her.

Exercises

Choose the best answer to each question.

1. The main difference between hot culture and cold culture lies in _____.
   A. the social structure
   B. the ruling value
   C. the areas where the culture rooted
   D. the religion

2. According to Lanier, people from hot cultures would center their life on _____.
   A. people and relations around them
   B. accomplishing tasks in time with a group
   C. hospitality when hosting friends
   D. carrying on religious believes

3. According to Lanier, people from cold cultures tend to _____.
   A. be selfish
   B. communicate more indirectly
   C. think more individualistically
   D. include others in their presence

4. Why does someone of a hot culture say "yes" when he actually wants to say "no"?
   A. Because he wants to make you feel good.
   B. Because he wants to preserve your relationship.

C. Because he feels rude saying "no."

D. All the above.

5. When a cold culture guest refuses your invitation, it may be because _____.

A. he doesn't want to come

B. your invitation is too late

C. he doesn't have time to give a reply

D. your invitation is not explicit

SECTION 6 CULTURAL EXPLORATION

In this section, you will learn Chinese etiquette from the cultural perspective.

Task 1 Understanding Chinese etiquette in ancient poems or famous quotes

Read and study the following ancient Chinese poem related to hosting guests in English and then find out its original Chinese version. What message is being conveyed in this poem?

To Guests (Excerpt)
From Book of Songs
By Anonymity
Translated by Xu Yuanchong

How gaily call the deer,
While eating southernwood!
I have welcome guests here,
Who give advices good.
My people are benign;
My lords will learn from you.
I have delicious wine;
You may enjoy my brew.

How gaily call the deer,
Eating grass in the shade!
I have welcome guests here.
Let lute and flute be played.
Play lute and zither fine;
We may enjoy out best.
I have delicious wine,

Unit 2 Hosting the Home Guests

To delight the heart of my guest.

作者_____
译者_____

_____
_____
_____
_____
_____
_____
_____
_____
_____
_____
_____
_____
_____
_____

Task 2 Learning Chinese traditions related to the etiquette of this unit

Read the following introduction to Tea-drinking in China and identify the major cultural points included in the passage. Then pick out some key words or cultural expressions that help you remember and understand the major points.

> Tea-drinking is a constituent part of Chinese culture. According to Chinese mythology, tea was discovered in about 2700 BC by Shennong, whose name literally means "Divine Farmer" and who is considered to have been one of the Three Sovereigns (also known as "Three Emperors"). He was considered the founder of ancient Chinese agriculture and ancient Chinese medicine and a combination of both led to the discovery of tea.
>
> It was his decree that all water should be boiled before drinking. So when the Emperor and his entourage on one of their travels stopped for a rest, he was handed a cup of boiled water. At that moment the wind blew a leaf from a nearby tree into his cup. Being a curious

man the Emperor allowed the leaf to steep in his cup for a while and after a few moments he noticed the water's color changing and a subtle aroma wafting from the cup. When he took a sip he enjoyed a delicate flavor and as he finished the cup he felt new energy and experienced clarity of mind. He ordered the magical tree which the leaf fell from be taken to his gardens and thus the cultivation of tea began.

Nowadays, with the popularization of tea, people in different regions and of different nationalities have developed their own unique custom of taking tea. In Guangdong, for example, people like drinking morning tea; in Fujian they prefer kongfu tea; Hunan has Lei tea; Sichuan people love "covered-bowl tea," while people of the Bai nationality treat their guests with "three-course tea." Tibetan people prefer buttered tea and those from Inner Mongolia like milk tea. These various tea customs constitute the rich and profound Chinese tea culture. Many traditional Chinese families drink tea after dinner or when greeting visitors. This is not only a healthy habit but also reflects rich culture and history. Chinese people can chat with a friend for a whole afternoon over a pot of good tea.

1. Major cultural points in the story:
   (1) _____
   (2) _____
   (3) _____
2. Major words or cultural expressions in the story:
   (1) Para. 1 _____
   (2) Para. 2 _____
   (3) Para. 3 _____
3. What interesting stories about Tea-drinking or other manners in hosting guests would you like to share with your classmates?

Unit 3
Dining Culture

You will learn in this unit
☐ good table manners
☐ ordering meals
☐ formal table setting

SECTION 1   INTRODUCTION

🎧 **Listen to the following passage and fill in the blanks.**

Through thousands of years of evolution, dining etiquette 1._____ a set of generally assumed rituals and practice, a cultural system 2._____ sociology, philosophy, aesthetics and health science, with variations in cooking habits and table manners in accordance with the character and purpose of the banquet and regional differences. By looking into 3._____ of dining etiquette, an increased inter-cultural awareness of being one 4._____ will definitely be achieved and a good knowledge of cross-cultural interaction principles will surely 5._____, with an emphasis on the confirmation of common core values of openness, 6._____, mutual understanding and mutual respect.

Dining etiquette 7._____ in almost all aspects of a dining activity like taking your seat, serving food, using utensils, starting and ending meals. Imagine you were invited to a formal dinner. What would you wear? What would you say? How would you behave? Whatever the occasion, social gatherings have long been 8._____ by etiquette—a way of living, based upon gentleness and kindliness, intended to make life better for all involved. While some of the rules have changed, it is still important to make a favorable impression and 9._____ to your dining companions. It is not just social etiquette for having a dinner party or business dinner—it is all about being the very 10._____, thinking about other people before yourself, behaving properly and in a way that you would want to be treated yourself.

SECTION 2   CHECK YOUR MANNERS

Read the following statements, then mark T for the true statements and F for the false statements. Provide corrections for the false ones.

___ 1.   If your fork falls on the floor, pick it up and clean it with your napkin.
___ 2.   When you have finished eating, refold your napkin to the way it was before and put it next to your plate.
___ 3.   You should excuse yourself if you leave the table during a meal.
___ 4.   You should stand up to get the salt if it is out of your reach.
___ 5.   Don't burp because it is considered rude.
___ 6.   Always use the water glass to your right.

___ 7. Keep your elbows off the table, especially when you are eating.

___ 8. Your bread and butter plate is located towards the left of an imaginary line across your service plate.

___ 9. When you finish your meal, put your fork and knife back on the table where they were before.

___ 10. If there are two forks on the table, you should start using the fork closest to the plate.

SECTION 3   PRACTICE

In this section, proper dining etiquette will be learned through different tasks.

Task 1   Naming the items
Work in pairs. Find out the right names of the following items and fill in the blanks.

1. _____   2. _____   3. _____

4. _____   5. _____   6. _____

7. _____   8. _____   9. _____

10. _____   11. _____   12. _____

13. _____   14. _____   15. _____

Task 2   Resetting the table
The formal table setting in Task 1 is not correct. Some items have been set in the wrong place. Work in pairs, and find out the items which are in the wrong place and put them in the right place.

Task 3 Dining with proper etiquette

Complete the conversations using expressions from the box, then role-play each conversation with a partner.

> saucer   a glass of Coke   something
> coaster   like to order   the tip of a clean knife
> quickly take a swallow of water   Chinese food
> have cold dishes and drinks   soup or tea
> and your mouth is scalding, should you spit it out   first

Conversation 1

Li Ming: How should one drink iced tea or coffee, Lily?
Lily: Preferably, iced tea and coffee are served in a glass placed on a 1._____ or 2._____.
Li Ming: How should one use salt in a saltcellar?
Lily: If there is no spoon in a saltcellar, use 3._____.
Li Ming: How should one handle food that is too hot?
Lily: If a bite of food is too hot 4._____. Only if there is no beverage 5._____.
Li Ming: Thanks a lot.

Conversation 2

Li Ming: What shall we order?
Lily: This is my first time in a Chinese restaurant. You order, please. Would you tell me how to eat 6._____ in a restaurant?
Li Ming: All right.
Waiter: Good evening, sir. Here is the menu. Would you 7._____ now or later?
Li Ming: Later please. But would you give me 8._____ or 9._____ to drink? I'm really thirsty.
Waiter: Ok. I'll come back in a few minutes.
Lily: Following the Chinese way, what should we have first?
Li Ming: You know, in a Chinese restaurant, people always 10._____ first, then hot dishes and rice. 11._____ is the last course.
Lily: Oh. That's really different from ours. We have tea or soup 12._____.

	It's called an appetizer. Then we'll order the entree. Excuse me, should we call the waiter now? You know, good food in a restaurant always makes my mouth water.
Li Ming:	Ah, I'm also feeling hungry. Let's talk more about it when the food comes.
Lily:	That's a good idea.

SECTION 4 CASE STUDY

Read the following cases and do each case study in small groups. The questions in "critical thinking" after each case are aimed to help with finding the story background, the problem itself, the etiquette involved, and the cultural differences behind the etiquette. Remember to provide possible solutions to the problem in each case.

Case 1

Dinner with Friends

Roger was a student majoring in East Asia Studies in an American university. He started an email correspondence with Li Zhang, a sociology major in China, who was introduced to him through a mutual friend.

Upon graduation, Roger got a big gift from his grandfather —Grandpa would pay for a round-trip ticket to China. He told Li Zhang the good news, and the two decided to meet. Li Zhang decided to give Roger a very special welcome: she and the three women students in her dormitory would cook him an authentic Chinese meal as Roger had told her that he loved Chinese food.

However, when Roger was present at the dinner, he was confused by some of the food: pork stomach soup, pig liver with ginger and spring onion, chicken with mushrooms in which the chicken had been cut into pieces with bones attached to the meat.

Fortunately, there were courses like bean curd, stirred fried beef, steamed fish and vegetables that Roger loved. He tried to stick to them, but Li Zhang kept putting food he did not like on his plate. When she asked how he liked the liver, Roger said, "It's very unusual … and interesting." This seemed to make Li Zhang happy and she gave him some more liver. Roger tried to stop her, but she would not be stopped. Roger was so frustrated that he told her that he did not really like it that much.

"But you said it was unusual and interesting!" Li Zhang said.

"Well, they both mean something less than positive," Roger said carefully, trying not to hurt their feelings.

Li Zhang and her friends became concerned at this. "So you don't like the food?"

"I'm not used to eating liver, that's all. But I do like the chicken, the beef, the bean curd, and the vegetables. I have had more than enough to eat. I never make this much food at home," Roger was eager to let them know how much he appreciated their effort. "Trust me, I'm enjoying the food. I know what I like."

Having said that, he found a piece of chicken that was less bony, held it in his hands to eat it, and then licked his fingers.

Li Zhang and her friends looked at each other in shock.

It was not a perfect first meeting for either Li Zhang or Roger.

Critical thinking

1. Retell the case in 3–4 sentences using the expressions in the box.

a special welcome	authentic	confuse	
unusual and interesting	appreciate	lick	shock

2. The last sentence of the case tells that it was not a perfect first meeting for either Li Zhang or Roger. Please list the misunderstandings between them and discuss in groups what you would do if you were Roger or Li Zhang to make this meeting a perfect one.

3. What etiquette do you attach great importance to when dining with friends and why?

Case 2

Hot Pot Dining: A Whirlwind Experience in London

Davy's recent visit to the London branch of a hot pot restaurant unveiled a world of flavors and took him on a **captivating** (迷人的) journey of taste and tradition.

Before indulging in the hot pot feast, he found himself in the delightful company of Vivi, a talented nail technician. As he waited for a table, Vivi offered a unique experience by **pampering**

(细心照顾) his little fingers with a fresh coat of nail polish. Opting for orange to match his vibrant scarf and green to complement his suit, Vivi skillfully transformed his nails into colorful accents.

At the restaurant, an extensive and ever-evolving menu awaited adventurous diners like Davy. From fine cuts of meat to an array of fresh fish, vibrant vegetables, and daring choices like tripe, tongue, and chicken feet, the restaurant catered to all **palates** (味觉，爱好). The sheer variety of ingredients was enough to make his head spin with excitement.

As he sat at the table, Davy was presented with fresh raw ingredients, encouraging him to cook his own food directly. It was a chance for his **culinary** (烹饪的，厨房的) prowess to be put to the test as he carefully selected the appropriate cooking time for each delicacy. The attentive waitstaff were ever-present, ready to lend a helping hand and guide him through this **gastronomic** (美食的) journey.

As the first bites of carefully cooked morsels met his palate, the true essence of hot pot came to life. It was a sensory explosion of flavors, combining the delicate interplay of spices, herbs, and broth with the freshness of the ingredients.

However, the surprises didn't end with the sizzling pots and **delectable** (美味的) broths. For a while, Davy found his fingers twisted awkwardly when struggling to pick up some food with a pair of chopsticks. The nearby waitstaff immediately came up to offer help and show him how to hold them and shared with him interesting stories about chopstick manners. This unexpected episode added a touch of comedy to the dining experience.

And then, the spotlight fell on the star of the show—the chicken foot. As skepticism gave way to curiosity, he took the plunge. Surprisingly, this jelly-like texture offered a unique taste, and the knuckle nestled within the foot brought a slightly peculiar element to the dish. The flavors unfolded like a symphony, straying from the anticipated poultry taste. Davy just wondered what would turn up to surprise him again.

To highlight this captivating experience, the restaurant treated its patrons to traditional Chinese entertainment. The noodle dance **enthralled** (使着迷) onlookers as skilled performers twirled and stretched dough, creating fascinating displays of culinary artistry. This spectacle was followed by the charming face-changing dance, known as *Bianlian*, where vibrant colors, energetic music, and highly skilled face-shifters combined to create a truly awe-inspiring performance.

"In conclusion," Davy says, "I warmly recommend the hot pot experience to all those seeking a remarkable dining adventure. With its rich history, communal atmosphere, tantalizing flavors, and even the chance for a pre-meal nail pampering, hot pot transcends cultural boundaries and opens up a world of culinary exploration. Embark on your own hot pot odyssey at the restaurant, and let the magic of this ancient tradition transport you to a realm of taste and togetherness."

Critical thinking

1. Retell the case in 7–8 sentences using the expressions in the box.

| captivating | delightful company | ever-present | explosion of flavors |
| twisted awkwardly | spotlight | enthralled | taste and togetherness |

2. What are the surprises that impress Davy during this dinner?

3. What do you think the hot pot dinner is characterized by in this case?

SECTION 5 READING FOR ETIQUETTE TIPS

Read the following passages and finish the exercises after each of the texts.

Passage 1

Table Etiquette and Manners in Western Culture

Table manners have always played an important part in making a favorable impression. Our actions at the table and while eating can be essential to how others perceive us and can even affect our professional success. In this article you are going to learn about some basic Table Etiquette and Manners in the West.

Table setting

Table setting is of great importance for Western-style meal, especially for formal occasions. The table should have a centerpiece that performs a solely decorative function. The centerpiece may be huge and, including candles, may extend the full length of the table. The centerpiece should be of low height, so as not to obstruct the vision of other diners.

Informal settings generally have fewer utensils and dishes but use a stereotyped layout based on more formal settings. Utensils are arranged in the order and the way a person will use them. Usually in Western culture, that means that the forks, bread plate, butter knife, and napkins are to the left, while knives, spoons, drinkware, cups and saucers are to the right, although the left-right order is reversed in a minority of countries.

Utensils are placed about one inch from the edge of the table, each one lining up at the base with the one next to it. Utensils on the outermost position are used first (for example, a salad fork and a soup spoon, then the dinner fork and dinner knife). The blade of the knife must face toward the plate. The glasses are positioned about an inch from the knives, also in the order of use: white wine, red wine, dessert wine, and water tumbler.

It is important to place the glassware or cup back in the same position after it has been used in order to maintain the visual presence of the table. To the left of this imaginary line all of the following will be placed: bread and butter plate (including small butter knife placed horizontally across the top of the plate), salad plate, napkin, and forks. Remembering the rule of "liquids on your right" and "solids on your left" will help in allowing you to quickly become familiar with the place setting.

Napkin use

Place your napkin on your lap, completely unfolded if it is a small luncheon napkin or in half, if it is a large dinner napkin. Typically, you want to put your napkin on your lap soon after sitting down at the table (but follow your host's lead). The napkin remains on your lap throughout the entire meal and should be used to gently blot your mouth when needed. If you need to leave the table during the meal, place your napkin on your chair as a signal to your server that you will be returning. The host will signal the end of the meal by placing his or her napkin on the table. Once the meal is over, you too should place your napkin neatly on the table to the right of your dinner plate.

Use of silverware

Choosing the correct silver from the variety in front of you is not as difficult as it may first appear. Starting with the knife, fork, or spoon that is farthest from your plate, work your way in, using one utensil for each course. Your dessert spoon and fork are above your plate or brought out with dessert. If you remember the rule to work from the outside in, you'll be fine.

There are two ways to use a knife and fork to cut and eat your food. They are the American style and the European or Continental style. Either style is considered appropriate. In the American style, one cuts the food by holding the knife in the right hand and the fork in the left hand with the fork tines piercing the food to secure it on the plate. Change your fork from your left to your right hand to eat, fork tines facing up. In the European style, the difference is your fork remains in your left hand, tines facing down, and the knife in your right hand. Simply eat the cut pieces of food by picking them up with your fork still in your left hand.

General table manners
- Chew with your mouth closed.

- Do not talk at a loud volume and do not make loud or unusual noises while eating.

- Refrain from burping, coughing, sneezing or blowing nose at the table. If you must do, you may request that action be excused.

- Never tilt back your chair while at the table. Sit in a relaxed and comfortable position, but do not "slouch."

- Always ask the host or hostess to be excused before leaving the table.

- Do not stare at anyone while he or she is eating. It is considered rude.

- Never talk on your phone or text a friend at the table. If an urgent matter arises, ask the host or hostess if you can be excused, and step away from table.

Exercises

Choose the best answer to each question.

1. On formal occasions, a centerpiece on the table is usually _____.
    A. fragrant flowers only for decorative purpose
    B. a small item only to occupy a little space
    C. huge and long to make the table look grand
    D. delicate but of low height so as not to obstruct the line of vision

2. Utensils are arranged in the order and the way a person will use them. When the diner is left-handed, _____.
    A. the forks are to the right and the knives are to the left
    B. the blade of the knife must face toward the right
    C. the handle of the butter knife must point toward the left
    D. the liquids are to the right and the solids are to the left

3. When using a napkin, there are some common rules such as _____.
    A. fold the napkin in half when placing it on your lap
    B. unfold the napkin just before sitting down at the table
    C. use the napkin to gently blot your mouth when needed
    D. place the napkin on your chair to signal the end of the meal

4. Using silverware at the table is not as difficult as it appears, just _____.
    A. remember to start with the fork that is farthest from your plate
    B. remember to work from the outside in and use utensils properly
    C. remember to ask for a dessert spoon and fork early if they are not on the table

Unit 3 Dining Culture

D. remember to follow the American style in America and the European style in Europe
5. Good table manners involve behaving appropriately all the time through out the meal, so _____.
   A. don't slouch, but don't be afraid to sit in a relaxed position to make yourself comfortable
   B. don't make any noise at the table especially when you are chewing
   C. go to the restroom if you can't refrain from burping or sneezing
   D. always excuse yourself before you have to talk on your phone at the table

Passage 2

Differences between Eastern and Western Eating Habits

There are different ways of dining all around the world. Different cultures, especially Eastern and Western cultures, have different ways of eating, cooking and serving food.

Eating both Eastern and Western cuisine was a part of my childhood in Singapore, Malaysia and Australia. Growing up I had many friends and family from Asian and Western backgrounds and we constantly ate each other's cuisines. Evidently there were noticeably different eating habits and food preferences between each other's cultures.

When we speak of Eastern or Asian cuisine, we usually think of dishes originating from the Asian region, maybe rice and noodle dishes. When we speak of Western cuisine, dishes such as bread, potatoes and pasta commonly come to mind. That said, for each cuisine there are a multitude of varying dishes in between as this world is so diverse.

Long-held traditions and stereotypes often influence how we eat, dine and drink. Other times our eating habits are simply shaped by the eating practices and types of food that we are familiar and comfortable with.

Eastern vs. Western Eating Habits
- Utensils. Eating with a fork and spoon is the norm in some Western cultures, and so is eating with a knife when a good chunk of meat is served. There can be unique utensils for each course of a meal, such as in French dining. While many of an Asian background eat withs fork and spoons, many also eat with chopsticks or eat with just their hands.

When I was a kid, my Chinese-Malaysian parents first taught me to eat with a fork and spoon, and later taught me how to use chopsticks. These days I use chopsticks whenever I eat Chinese food; it just feels natural (probably from having watched my family eat Chinese food with only chopsticks as a kid). I have never had trouble picking up rice with chopsticks (which is baffling to some, but the trick is to put the rice bowl close to your mouth so rice doesn't fall everywhere).

● Table and seating configuration. Dining at round tables is common in Asian cultures and encourages inclusivity no matter where one sits. Dining at a round table, everyone can see each other—it encourages everyone to chat and connect with each other (one can see everyone at the table face to face). It's convenient to pass food around on a Lazy Susan in the middle of the table. Also, the eldest or most senior person usually takes the seat facing the entrance, symbolic of hierarchical respect.

Eating at rectangular tables is more common in Western cultures. One might not get the chance to chat with every single person when seated at this kind of table but might be highly encouraged to make small talk with the person beside or right in front of them.

● Sharing v. individual dishes. In Chinese culture most dishes are designed to be shared, and rice and noodles are supposed to be eaten along with these dishes. Everyone gets to try everything and this is **synonymous** (同义的) with the virtues of sharing and being a part of a group.

Individual dishes are more common in Western cultures and it's not surprising for someone to order one dish and have it all to themselves. On the plus side, when everyone orders a dish for themselves, it can be easier when it's time to pay the bill: everyone eats their own share, and pays for their own dish, no need to fight over the bill.

● Balance and variety. There is usually a starter/entrée, main and dessert when it comes to having many a Western meal. Sometimes this includes a salad and cheese course. While multicourse meals are also part of Asian dining, balance is key here: there is usually a soup, rice or noodles and a vegetable and meat dish served. With Asian cuisine, there is a focus on optimizing meals for digestion—aligning with the concept of yin and yang—rather than stuffing oneself and feeling **satiated** (吃饱喝足的).

● Flavours. Many Asian dishes are bold and **aromatic** (芳香的) in flavor. It's the ingredients used that bring out these flavors, ingredients such as vinegar, five spice powder, cooking wine, hoisin sauce and soy sauce. Ginger and garlic are also staple ingredients in many Chinese dishes, and there's usually the option of added chilli too. Compared to Asian cooking, Western cuisine might come across as blander. Chilli isn't served with every meal and many chilli dishes in Australia for example aren't as spicy as dishes in Asia. Processed sauces seemed to be served more with Western food. Tomato sauce, mustard, **mayonnaise** (蛋黄酱), and barbecue sauce are some popular sauces one finds with American, European and Australian cuisine.

Exercises

Choose the best answer to each question.

1. According to the passage, what would influence people's dining habits?

    A. Long-held traditions.

    B. Eating practices.

    C. Types of food.

    D. All the above.

2. In Western culture, _____.

    A. there can be unique utensils for each course of a meal, such as in French dining

    B. silver utensils are common at most dining events

    C. forks and spoons are the most frequently used utensils

    D. there can be situations where people eat rice with their hands

3. According to the passage, dining at round tables in Asian cultures gives people the feeling of _____.

    A. reverence for other diners

    B. intimacy with other diners

    C. inclusivity no matter where one sits

    D. hospitality no matter whom they dine with

4. According to the author, Asian cuisine focuses on _____.

    A. stuffing oneself

    B. making advantage of meals for balance inside the body

    C. the variety of the ingredients

    D. the flavor of the ingredients

5. Many Asian dishes are bold and **aromatic** (芳香的) in flavor because Asian people tend to _____.

    A. use special ingredients when cooking

    B. use processed sauces when cooking

    C. use sweet chilli when cooking

    D. use a secret recipe when cooking

SECTION 6 CULTURAL EXPLORATION

In this section, you will learn Chinese etiquette from the cultural perspectives.

Task 1 Understanding Chinese etiquette in ancient poems or famous quote

Read and study the following ancient Chinese poems related to cuisines in English and then find out their original Chinese versions. What messages are being conveyed in these poems?

Poem 1

> **The Fisherman on the Stream**
> *By Fan Zhongyan*
> *Translated by Xu Yuanchong*
>
> You go up and down stream;
> You love to eat the bream.
> Lo! The fishing boat braves
> Perilous wind and waves.
>
> _____
>
> 作者_____
> 译者_____
>
> _____
> _____
> _____

Poem 2

> **River Scenes on a Spring Evening**
> *By Su Shi*
> *Translated by Xu Yuanchong*
>
> Beyond bamboos a few twigs of peach blossoms blow;
> When spring has warmed the stream, ducks are the first to know.
> By water side short reeds bud and wild flowers teem;
> It is just time for the globefish to swim upstream.
>
> _____
> 作者_____

译者_____

_____
_____
_____
_____

Task 2 Learning Chinese traditions related to the etiquette of this unit

Read the following introduction to chopsticks in Chinese food culture and identify the major cultural points included in the passage. Then pick out some key words or cultural expressions that help you remember and understand the major points.

> Chopsticks, or *kuaizi*, are the most important eating utensils in China. Chinese use them during each meal every day. They consist of two sticks made from wood or bamboo and use the theory of leverage to pick up food. Westerners might be amazed when they watch Chinese use them to pick up meat balls, peanuts and beans so skillfully and leisurely and then put them into mouth so easily.
>
> Manners are important when using chopsticks just like using knives and forks in the West. You don't play with your chopsticks, like using them to purposefully hit on bowls, plates or cups to make a noise at the table, nor do you insert your chopsticks vertically into a bowl of rice or other food. Today serving chopsticks are being preferred when someone is offering to pick up some food for another diner at the same table. In brief, limit your use of chopsticks to picking up your own food and not to serve others.
>
> Chinese have used chopsticks for at least 3000 years. They have been spread to other Asian countries like Japan and Korea. The materials come from nature, which represents the wisdom of the Chinese—being warm and gentle instead of being cold and aggressive, being in harmony instead of being in hostility. In addition to being utensils for daily meals, ornate chopsticks are also being made today by skillful craftsman and being presented to newly-weds as wedding gifts delivering good wishes for "having kids soon," which again originates from some Chinese traditions.

1. Major cultural points in the story:

    (1) _____
    (2) _____
    (3) _____

2. Major words or cultural expressions in the story:
   (1) Para. 1 _____
   (2) Para. 2 _____
   (3) Para. 3 _____
3. What interesting stories about chopsticks or other tableware would you like to share with your classmates?

Unit 4
Behaving in Academic Situations

You will learn in this unit
- [ ] behaving well in classrooms
- [ ] communicating with instructors
- [ ] good manners in campus

SECTION 1 INTRODUCTION

🎧 **Listen to the following passage and fill in the blanks.**

Everyone who studies abroad faces some challenges. According to some 1._____ studies on Asian students studying overseas, language is not the only 2._____ they encounter. What they face can be 3._____ under three headings: academic life, social life and personal life.

For example, Asian students who are used to listening quietly to their teachers in class cannot quickly involve themselves into the atmosphere of a 4._____ class in North American universities since they are used to keeping silent instead of openly expressing themselves in public. In the communication between teachers and students, there are also great cultural differences in the 5._____ of teacher-student relationships. This brings a lot of confusion for Asian students. So, how should they address an 6._____? Is it okay to send an informal email to your professor just because he seems to be a very easy-going "guy" in class?

Although the world has been fully 7._____ in all aspects, people's 8._____ cultural system and values still deeply influence people's behavior. To be successful in overseas study, students still need to fully learn these differences and 9._____ them in their life abroad.

This unit will help learners understand what "academic 10._____" is, learn how to practice good manners on campus and how to deal with teacher-student relationship as an international student.

SECTION 2 CHECK YOUR MANNERS

Read the following questions, then tick the correct answer for each of them.

1. The instructor David Johnson of your math class got his Ph.D. from UCLA and holds the title of Associate Professor. Which of the following is NOT a correct way to address him?
   A. Doctor Johnson.
   B. Professor Johnson.
   C. Teacher Johnson.

2. If you are late for class or a meeting, what's the best way to deal with the situation?
   A. Nod to your instructor/host, say "Excuse me," and slip into the first available seat.

B. Go up to your instructor/host, say "I'm awfully sorry," and explain why you are late for the class.

   C. Stay outside and then leave because you are afraid of disturbing others.

3. If you absolutely must leave class/conference before the expected time, you _____.

   A. pack up your backpack, put your jacket on and slip out of the back door

   B. think it is a waste of time and leave while the speaker is still speaking

   C. leave during the break time

4. After an absence, you _____.

   A. ask an instructor, "Did I miss anything?"

   B. say sorry to your instructor, and borrow the notes from your classmates

   C. send an email to your instructor and ask for copies of his teaching notes

5. Which of the following is a proper description of a student's responsibility?

   A. You should email your instructor to ask "Will this be tested in the final exam?"

   B. You should ask your instructor whether it could be possible to give you a make-up quiz if you have missed one.

   C. If you fail to submit your work in time, you say, "It's my fault. Next time I won't do that."

6. Which of the following is an appropriate order to prepare for a class presentation?

   A. Analyze the assignment → make a PPT → organize your content → write a draft

   B. Analyze the assignment → make a PPT → write a speech draft → recite your draft → rehearse your presentation

   C. Analyze the assignment → collect information → organize your content → make a PPT → rehearse your presentation

7. Which of the following is a proper manner in a class or conference presentation?

   A. You try to write what you would say on your slides in case you forget them when you deliver a speech.

   B. You always use professional expressions to make sure that the information is conveyed exactly.

   C. When participating in a group presentation, you always introduce the next speaker to make your group presentation go smoothly.

8. As a presenter in a conference presentation, which of the following is not your job in the Q and A session?

   A. Clarify your answers if the asker is still in doubt.

   B. Introduce yourself properly.

   C. Invite questions from the audience.

9. In which of the following situations is it reasonable for a student to send an email to his professor?

   A. You are not satisfied with your grade for your math, and you want your professor to give you a higher score.

B. You are in trouble.

C. You ask for syllabus at the very beginning of a semester.

10. Which of the following demonstrates one's professionalism on campus or among academic peers?

   A. Professor Blair wrote an email with many abbreviations to his colleagues.

   B. Professor Smith blamed one of his students for sending an email to him and forwarding it to the whole class.

   C. Professor White uses direct, brief and specific language in professional emails.

SECTION 3 PRACTICE

In this section, you will learn some proper etiquette through different tasks.

Task 1 Communicating with your instructors appropriately

There are some situations in which you are required to communicate with your instructors appropriately (in terms of how and where). Suppose you are in the following situations, what are you going to do/say? Work in pairs and practice the etiquette.

Situation 1: Challenge an instructor's policy, grade, or assignment.

Situation 2: Ask for a(n) ill/business leave.

Situation 3: Leave the classroom early.

Situation 4: Want to a talk with your instructor but he is quite busy right now.

Situation 5: Tell your instructor that you need him to repeat what he just mentioned.

Task 2 Composing your first email

When applying to a school, it is often a good idea to write a short email to professors who are doing work you may be interested in. The first email you send to a professor is the initial contact you will have with him or her. As such, it should be well-written and to the point. Most professors are very helpful and happy to help interested students understand more about the program or the professors' particular research interests. Now, suppose you are composing your first email to a professor whose work you admire.

1. What might be the componental elements you will include? Tick the possible items.

   (1) Your interest in his/her work

   (2) Some of your salient features

Unit 4   Behaving in Academic Situations

   (3) What has motivated you to apply
   (4) What you are studying
   (5) Who you are
   (6) Your appreciation for his/her time and attention
   (7) Your name
   (8) Subject in the subject line
   (9) Your email address
   (10) Some brief questions

2. Put your selected items into a good order.

   _____

3. Extend this outline into an email with a good form.

   [   ]

Once you have sent the email, allow up to a week for a response before you send another one. The most common reason why the professors do not respond quickly is that they are very busy with conferences, research or travel, not that they don't want to talk to you.

Task 3 Making your decisions on the following situations

Work in pairs and decide what you should do in the following situations. Give your answers using one sentence.

1. You have an appointment to see your adviser at 10:30 tomorrow morning, but you have a fever now and are too sick to keep your appointment. What should you do?

   _____

2. You have not done well on a paper, and your professor has called you into his office to talk to you about your poor grade. When he speaks to you, what should you do?

3. You have been doing well in all your classes except social studies. You have the feeling that the teacher doesn't like you. What should you do?

4. You don't like to answer or ask questions in class. But your teacher has claimed that class participation accounts for 30% of your final grade. What should you do?

5. Your teacher has just announced an important test for Friday, but you have a very important appointment that day. What should you do?

Task 4 Evaluating and improving your performance in a class presentation

1. Please make a video of yourself doing a presentation to introduce your hometown. Then share your video with your group members and ask three peers to evaluate your performance by using the checklist in the following table. You should evaluate your own work as well before you take a look at their comments. Compare the comments and see whether others agree with you.

No.	Items for description	Poor	Average	Good
1	Confident voice			
2	Natural gestures			
3	Appropriate appearance			
4	Proper visual aids			
5	No distraction in the items 1–4			
6	Greetings to the audience			
7	Logical organization			
8	Impressive final remarks			
9	Listener-friendly design in the items 6–8			
10	Sense of communication			
Overall comments				

Unit 4   Behaving in Academic Situations

2. Discuss in a small group about how you can improve your performance in your presentation. Make another video about the same topic. This time, see how much you've improved. Write down your reflections in the following box.

Task 5   Q and A session in academic context

1. Q and A session is not only an essential part for a speaker to prepare for, but also a useful technique for a qualified attendee of various academic sessions, such as a lecture, a seminar, a conference presentation, or even a class instruction. There are different types of questions you could ask on an academic occasion. Think of questions of the following types concerning one of the presentations your group members have done in task 4. When you have thought of your questions, practice asking them to your peers in the following class activities.

Questions for clarifying points	
Questions for getting additional information	
Questions for raising different opinions	
Questions for asking for comments/suggestions	
Questions for comprehensive examinations	
Questions for other complicated reasons	

2. Both question raisers and speakers should adopt some strategies to ask or answer questions in a professional manner. Go through the tips in asking questions and answering questions, and be ready to employ these strategies later.

When asking questions, you should:	When answering questions, you should:
· Introduce yourself.	· Choose your questioners.
· Show appreciation or compliment.	· Listen carefully to the questions.
· Specify your theme.	· Acknowledge the question.
· Ask your question.	· Respond clearly and briefly.
· Clarify and check comprehension.	· Check the feedback.
· Respond to answers (satisfactory or unsatisfactory).	· Allow for follow-ups.

3. Practice asking and answering questions in your group in turn.

SECTION 4   CASE STUDY

Read the following cases and do each case study in small groups. The questions in "Critical thinking" after each case are aimed to help with finding the story background, the problem itself, the etiquette involved, and the cultural differences behind the etiquette. Remember to provide possible solutions to the problem in each case.

Case 1

Meeting with a Professor

I am meeting with a biology professor to discuss opportunities for an undergraduate RA. I initiated the contact by introducing myself via email and sending him my CV and general areas of interest. He agreed to meet with me to discuss research opportunities, but I am wondering what the expected length of a meeting like this should be. Also, are there any documents (e.g. printed copy of my CV) that I should bring? Should I come prepared with questions about his research (which would require hours and hours of reading, because while his work seems interesting to me, it's also very difficult to fully understand) or simply honestly tell him that I'm not as knowledgeable about his work as I would like to be but it sounds very interesting to me and I want to be involved? Lastly, is there any dress code for such a meeting?

Unit 4 Behaving in Academic Situations

Critical thinking

1. Look up the following words and abbreviations and explain them to your partner.

   (1) undergraduate

   (2) RA

   (3) CV

   (4) dressing code

2. Describe the author's problems in your own words.

3. Discuss the questions raised by the author and express your opinion in a small group.

Case 2

Cultural Difference in Academic Communication

A. An international student Sue wanted to ask her American tutor to do her a favor.

   Sue: Are you very busy?

   The tutor: Yes, this is a busy time for me.

   And then Sue went off. She was so disappointed because her expectation was that the tutor would respond with: "What's up?"

B. Sue was planning to pay a visit to her academic advisor Professor Johnson this afternoon.

   Sue: Are you free this afternoon?

   Prof. Johnson: … (Maybe he was thinking "It's none of your business.")

C. Sue was writing an application letter to the university she was interested in. Her letter started like this:

   To whom it may concern:

   My name is Sue and I'm 21 years old. I will graduate from _____ University this summer and my major is_____.

   In my four years' study here, I participated _____ and was a member of _____.

   …

   …

   …

   Last year, I got a chance to read Professor Johnson's article about _____, and I was so impressed by _____.

   So, I'm writing to apply for the graduate program _____.

Looking forward to hearing from you.
Thank you for your time and attention.

Sue

Critical thinking

1. Please role-play situation A and B using proper manner and language and explain why you perform in that way.

2. Work in a group to revise the letter in part C and get ready to share your revised version in class. You have to explain the reasons for your revision.

3. Are westerners always direct and straightforward? If so why?

Case 3

What Is the Cultural Problem?

Mindy had heard when she was in her home country that North American teachers are very relaxed, that they tell jokes and call students by their first name. She had also heard that teachers dress informally. She thought it would be fun to study in the United States, but she wasn't prepared for what happened to her the first week in class.

On her first day at school, Mindy was surprised to see her teacher sitting on the desk. Her teacher told the students her name was Barbara and when Mindy said, "Miss Barbara, what is the assignment?" Barbara laughed and said, "My first name is Barbara. I'm Barbara Kelly. Just call me Barbara. We never use Mr., Mrs., or Miss with a first name." Everyone laughed. Mindy felt uncomfortable.

The next day they were talking about differences between cultures. Each student had to tell something that he or she would never say when meeting with people for the first time.

One student, Ann, said that she would never ask people how old they were. Another student, Jennifer, said she wouldn't ask people how much money they earned. Then the teacher asked Mindy what people couldn't say in her country.

The teacher looked at her and said, "Could you say, 'My, you have a fat mother!'" Everyone laughed. Mindy's face turned red and she looked down at the ground.

Barbara said, laughingly, "Well, could you say that?" She looked kindly at Mindy with a big smile on her face, but Mindy didn't see her because she was looking at the floor.

Mindy didn't answer and kept looking down. The class was still laughing. Finally, Mindy whispered "No."

The next day, Mindy went to the registrar's office and dropped Barbara's class. She really wanted to go home.

Critical thinking

1. Retell the case in 3–4 sentences using the expressions in the box.

north Americans	relaxed	fun
surprised	first name	cultural differences
meeting others	for the first time	laughed
turn red	look down	embarrassed
drop class		

2. North American teachers are very relaxed, friendly, easy-going and humorous. Is that true? Why did Barbara ask Mindy those questions? What was she expecting? Why did Mindy decide to drop the class?

3. Is that normal for a teacher to sit on a desk when teaching in China? What would a Chinese teacher do in such situation? What is the difference? Why is there such a difference?

SECTION 5 READING FOR ETIQUETTE TIPS

Read the following passages and finish the exercises after each of the texts.

Passage 1

A Student's Guide to Academic Etiquette

Addressing instructors

Students should avoid calling their instructors by first names (and should avoid asking permission to do so). Using the title "Professor" is always appropriate and preferable to "Mr.," "Ms.," or "Mrs." If a syllabus indicates the instructor has earned a Ph.D., using the title "Doctor" is equally appropriate.

Annoying questions and assertions

In conversations with their instructors, students should consider the appropriateness of the following questions or of **assertions** (要求，主张):

"I missed class the other day. Did I miss anything important? Oh. Well, can you go over everything I may have missed?"

"Do you have a stapler or paper clip for my paper?"

"I have to have an 'A' in this course. You're the only professor who is hurting my GPA."

"I have to work over forty hours a week. You cannot expect me to spend much time on assignments."

"Why don't you grade me on my effort even though I failed the test?"

Assignments

Instructors expect students to consider all assignments as serious extensions of in-class instruction rather than as **punitive** (惩罚性的) "busy work." Students should allow a minimum of two or three hours of study and assignments for every one hour of a course's credit hour. In other words, students should expect to spend roughly six to nine hours a week for each three-hour credit course they take. Stapled homework or essays are preferable to "dog-eared" papers. All submissions should include the course and section number.

Attendance

In the workplace, employers expect and rely upon regular work hours. Similarly, unless students are enrolled in non-traditional courses not requiring regular classroom attendance, instructors expect regular attendance and **timeliness** (时间性) to be crucial components of positive outcomes. Notifying instructors of an anticipated absence is always appropriate.

Authority

At times, some students may want to challenge an instructor's policy, grade, or assignment. First, they should consider the time, manner, and place. The instructor's office, not the classroom during a lecture, is always an appropriate setting—just as a non-argumentative tone is an appropriate one.

Civility

Civility is the **underpinning** (基础) of all the subject headings of this guide. To enhance the quality of education by avoiding behaviors **obstructing** (妨碍) learning opportunities, students must recognize that increasing diversity in the classroom demands increasing efforts to maintain mutual respect, tolerance of differences, and reasoned discourse. A healthy debate can energize and enrich everyone.

Entering and exiting

Students entering the classroom late should take a seat close to the door instead of walking in front of the instructor to take a seat. If a seat near the door is unavailable, they should at the least walk behind the instructor to get to a desk. They should not expect a **reiteration**(重申) of missed instruction (students who arrive late should instead wait until class is over to ask their peers about missed instruction). Students who know in advance they must leave class early should arrive to class early enough to take a seat near the door as well as to inform the instructor. Students who unexpectedly leave class should avoid walking in front of their instructors.

Note-taking and tape recorders

All instructors assume their students have developed good note-taking skills. (Students whose note-taking skills are weak should consider taking a note-taking skills seminar.) Arriving to class without a **notepad** (记事本) and pen is irresponsible. Assuming that everything an instructor says is noteworthy should prevent students from asking whether or not to take notes. Equally if not more important is developing a daily habit of reviewing class notes. Finally, students must get their instructor's permission before recording a lecture.

Office hours

All full-time faculty usually post office hours in their syllabuses and on their office doors. If students cannot visit their instructors during regular office hours, they should make arrangements to meet at other mutually convenient times. The office, not the classroom, is the appropriate place to discuss personal issues, such as upcoming surgical dates, requests for reference letters, and assignment difficulties. Further, students who have missed class should not expect a reiteration of instruction. They should also respect their instructor's time by not chatting at the desk just as the instructor is starting to address the class (or when class is over instead of letting the instructor leave the classroom for other duties).

Participation

Participation in class discussions, in group work, and in field work is a vital part of a college education. Students should engage fully in class discussions and **collaborative** (协作性的) assignments. They should also not rely on others to do the work, then claim credit for doing the work themselves. Finally, students should avoid pretending to have read an assignment; an admission of failure to do an assignment is better than attempts at bluffing with made-up responses.

Personal questions

At times, students may wish to know about their instructors' personal lives. If instructors do not volunteer private information, however, students should assume personal **intrusions** (入侵) are unwelcome.

Responsibility

Students who miss class should not expect the instructor to supply the missed instruction. Instead, students should get necessary information from other students. Should students have to miss class on a day an assignment is due, they are responsible for getting their assignments turned in on time by other means.

Exercises

Choose the best answer to each question.

1. Assignments are all the following except _____.

    A. a serious extension of in-class instruction

    B. a punishment

    C. part of a credit course

    D. well-stapled essays

2. When challenging your teacher for any reason, you should do it _____.

    A. in the classroom during a lecture

    B. in the office when it is office hours

    C. via mail or e-mail only

    D. in an argumentative or defensive tone

3. According to the text, civility doesn't mean _____.

    A. mutual respect

    B. tolerance of differences

    C. reasoned discourse

    D. emotional hostility

4. Which one is correct about note-taking?

    A. Note-taking is not an essential skill for all the students.

    B. You should ask for permission if you want to record the class using any digital devices.

    C. Every word the teacher said in class is important to note down.

    D. Note-taking does not need practicing at all.

5. Participation means _____.

    A. you should keep silent in class discussion

    B. you take credit without doing anything for a group work

    C. you should contribute your ideas in group work

    D. you could rely on other members because you are in a group

Passage 2

Academic Email Etiquette

Emailing a scholar in your field can be a **daunting** (令人退缩的) task. Whether you're a postgraduate student looking for a supervisor for your **dissertation** (论文) or an industry professional looking for a collaborative work opportunity, knowing proper academic email etiquette can help you make a great first impression. In this guide, you will be provided with some tips on email etiquette, planning, and getting the response you're looking for.

Do your research

Before you begin, take the time to identify your goals and compile a list of scholars whose interests and fields of **expertise** (专业知识) match them. Be sure to review some of their past projects and publications and take notes on items that you found interesting, as these details can be used when constructing your email to show your commitment to your work. Lastly, determine what their present **foci** (焦点) are.

Introduce yourself (and your purpose)

After crafting a **succinct** (简洁的) subject line and a **salutation** (问候), it's time to introduce yourself and the purpose of your email.

Proper email etiquette recommends that you provide a few lines about yourself, and the information included will depend on the purpose of your email. For simple requests, such as for a copy of a scholar's published work, it would be sufficient to include your name, profession, and **affiliation** (从属关系), as well as the reason for your request. In some cases, it could be beneficial to compliment the **recipient** (收件人) on their area of expertise to show them why you're interested in speaking with them as opposed to someone else.

Create a closing line

After introducing yourself and your purpose, it's time to conclude your email. This is the last item that a scholar will read, and it can motivate their decision to respond to you quickly—or at all. The last line of your email should not only express gratitude to the recipient for reading it, but should also invite a response. This communicates your expectations and helps you establish further communication.

In the context of professional email etiquette, expressing gratitude can be as simple as saying "Thank you for your time and consideration" or "I sincerely appreciate your guidance." It's an opportunity to thank the scholar for assisting you with a task or considering you for a position. A little politeness goes a long way!

How you make sure that you get a response will depend on the nature of your goal. For simpler requests, establishing a **rapport** (和谐关系) may not be necessary; however, it could prove useful in the future if you wish to pursue the scholar's area of interest further, or if you have a genuine interest in their work. For more complex requests, this relationship would give you the opportunity to show your dedication to the subject and your excitement toward discussing it further. In short, determine how much you want to invest in this (potential) relationship, and **craft** (精巧制作) your request for a response accordingly.

In line with proper email etiquette, each **scenario** (场景) and relationship **dictates** (规定) what is appropriate. Given the context of meeting someone for the first time, it would be best to invite them to email you back or to call to discuss your request further. You could also invite them to meet in a professional setting, such as a conference, if you know they'll be attending. Do not, however, invite them to your home or offer to visit them at theirs. Below is an example of an appropriate closing line.

I would love to discuss this position more with you. Please feel free to email or call me at your earliest convenience.

Sign off with an academic email signature

After your closing line, it's time to conclude your email. Be sure to include a **valediction** (告别), your full name, your current role, and your contact information.

• Valedictions. There are many valedictions (or "sign offs") to choose from when composing an email, and all of them serve different functions. For example, "**cordially** (诚挚的)," "take care," "love," "cheers" are perceived as more personal or informal; while "sincerely," "regards," "your sincerely," "kind regards" are viewed as professional enough. In an academic context, you're emailing a professor or a scholar whom you do not know; therefore, it follows that you would like to use a sign off that is professional without being too personal.

• Your name and professional title. When signing off, use your full name. This will prevent confusion and help them remember you. Including your full name in your email signature can also increase your chances of receiving a response and decrease your chances of having your email lost in a spam filter.

While it's not always necessary, it is recommended that you add your professional title or current role to your email signature; it helps illustrate what you do. If a scholar can see that you're affiliated with a reputable workplace or educational institution, they may be more inclined to take you seriously and/or honor your request.

Unit 4 Behaving in Academic Situations

● Provide additional contact information. Lastly, ensure that you add your contact information. While the scholar will be receiving your email address via the email, it's helpful to add other methods of communication, such as a direct telephone number. It's also nice to give the recipient options for communication, as some individuals have preferences. For example:

Kind regards,
Inigo Montoya

Ph.D. candidate
Department of Medieval Studies
Yale University
Email: inigo.montoya@yale.com
Phone: (123) 555-1234

Conclusion

While emailing a scholar can be stressful, it doesn't have to be. With a little research and planning, you can craft a perfect professional message for your intended audience and achieve your goals.

Exercises

Choose the best answer to each question.

1. What should you do before you contact a scholar by sending an email?
    A. Identify your goal or purpose of contacting.
    B. Review some of his/her projects.
    C. Read through some of his/her publications.
    D. All of the above.
2. Which of the following is not necessary when you introduce yourself to the email recipient?
    A. Your basic information.
    B. Your affiliation.
    C. Your hobbies.
    D. Your reasons of contacting.
3. The functions of the last line of your email include the following except _____.
    A. requesting a response
    B. establishing good relationship
    C. showing you gratitude
    D. restating your purpose

4. Which of the following is the best description of the elements you include in your concluding part of your email?

   A. Your valediction, your given family name, your position, your affiliation.

   B. Your valediction, your full name, your contact information.

   C. Your organization, your family name.

   D. Your title, your mailbox information, your given name.

5. Which of the following is not the reason why you are recommended to include your current role or your professional title?

   A. The recipient may get a hint of your affiliation.

   B. The recipient may consider that it is easier to get in contact with you.

   C. The recipient may be more likely to respond to you.

   D. The recipient may take you more seriously.

SECTION 6 CULTURAL EXPLORATION

In this section, you will learn Chinese etiquette from the cultural perspective.

Task 1 Understanding Chinese etiquette in ancient poems or famous quotes

Read and study the following ancient Chinese scripture related to learning in English and then find out its original Chinese version. What message is being conveyed in this scripture?

> **About Learning (Also known as "Record on the Subject of Education")**
> *From* Book of Rites
> *Translated by James Legge*
>
> However fine the viands be,
> if one do not eat,
> he does not know their taste;
> however perfect the course may be,
> if one do not learn it,
> he does not know its goodness.
> Therefore when he learns,
> one knows his own deficiencies;
> when he teaches,
> he knows the difficulties of learning.
> After he knows his deficiencies,

one is able to turn round and examine himself;

after he knows the difficulties,

he is able to stimulate himself to effort.

_____

作者_____
译者_____

_____
_____
_____
_____
_____
_____
_____
_____
_____
_____
_____

Task 2 Learning Chinese traditions related to the etiquette of this unit

Read the following short passage about respecting teachers in China and identify the major cultural points included in it. Then pick out some key words or cultural expressions that help you remember and understand the major points.

> Though the observance of Teacher's Day on Sep.10th itself is a modern tradition, China actually has a long history of respecting teachers. In ***Discourses of the States*** (《国语》), a historical book believed to be the work of historian **Zuo Qiuming** (左丘明) in the Spring and Autumn Period (770 BC–476 BC), a folk saying was recorded which states: "**One should serve their father, their teacher, and their monarch until death, because their father gave life to them, their teacher educated them, and their monarch provided food for them** (民生于三，事之如一。父生之，师教之，君食之。)." Similarly, Qing Dynasty scholar **Luo Zhenyu** (罗振玉) wrote: "**Students should treat their teacher with**

> **the same respect as they treat their father … even if someone just teaches you for one day, you should respect him like your father all your life**（弟子事师，敬同于父……一日为师，终身为父。）."
>
> Honoring teachers and appreciating their intellect has always been a tradition in China. Teachers have been respected by people as messengers of wisdom.
>
> The famous Chinese idiom, "Cheng Men Li Xue," which literally means "standing in the snow at the gate of Cheng's home," is a wonderful example. "Cheng" refers to Cheng Yi, one of the leading philosophers of Neo-Confucianism in the Song Dynasty (960–1276). Attracted by Cheng's theory, Yang Shi, a talented, hardworking young man who loved reading and studying, worshipped Cheng as his mentor.
>
> One day, Yang and his friend You Zuo had different opinions on one question. In order to get a proper answer, they went to Cheng's home for advice.
>
> It was in the middle of winter. Feeling frozen by the wind and snow, the two men wrapped themselves tightly in their clothes and hurried on. When they arrived at Cheng's place, the gatekeeper said the master was taking a nap.
>
> The two students did not complain. Instead, they chose not to disturb the teacher and waited outside the door, standing in heavy snowfall.
>
> After quite some time, Cheng upon waking up became aware that his students had been standing still in the snow for quite a while and immediately invited them to come in. By this time, the snowfall was already one foot thick.
>
> Deeply moved by Yang's patience, Cheng gave detailed answers to the students' questions. After years of study, Yang finally achieved his life goal as a great scholar.

1. Major cultural points in the story:

    (1) _____
    (2) _____
    (3) _____

2. Major words or cultural expressions in the story:

    (1) Para. 1 _____
    (2) Para. 2 _____
    (3) Para. 3 _____

3. What interesting stories about teacher-student relationship would you like to share with your classmates?

Unit 5
Making Telephone Calls

You will learn in this unit
- [ ] basic telephone etiquette
- [ ] handling phone calls expertly when at work
- [ ] using mobile phone appropriately
- [ ] displaying courtesy on the telephone communication

SECTION 1 INTRODUCTION

🎧 **Listen to the following passage and fill in the blanks.**

Whether you work in the retail trade or in the IT business, in a restaurant or in an administrative office, phone calls are 1._____. The phone conversations people have with you will 2._____ of you and your office (or your company). Good telephone etiquette means being respectful to the person you are talking with, showing consideration for the other person's limitations, allowing that person time to speak, communicating clearly and 3._____ the phone politely. Besides these traditional telephone manners, the subject of modern mobile manners is 4._____ at the best of times when mobile technology is developing very fast. This is the modern challenge we face. Smartphones are a 5._____, performing several functions in our work and private lives. In other words: Wherever we go, they go. Our 6._____ of technology provides the perfect platform for us to slip up when it comes to traditional manners, and our consistent use of it means there's plenty of opportunity to do so. Bad mobile habits might 7._____ 93% of smartphone users, and it even gets worse on business occasions where business mobile phone etiquette 8._____ and expects highly professional practice in phone use. When it comes to 9._____ our mobile manners, it's important to keep in mind that 10._____ should always be the dominant virtue.

SECTION 2 CHECK YOUR MANNERS

Choose the best answer for each of the following questions or situations.

1. What does not need to be considered before you make a phone call?
   A. The purpose of your call.
   B. The best time to call.
   C. A brief joke to break the ice.

2. What is not an active listening word that will let your party know you are listening while on a business phone call?
   A. "What?"
   B. "I see."
   C. "Great."

3. Why should you generally not answer your business phone on the first ring?
   A. It's rude.
   B. You don't look busy enough.

C. It can catch the caller off-guard.
4. If you need to discuss sensitive issues over the phone (including exchanges of personal and protected information), how should you handle it with your phone companion?

   A. Confirm with them it's ok to discuss before discussing it.

   B. Tell them you'll email it.

   C. Avoid these discussions at all costs on the telephone.

5. You are told to get the company representative in the San Francisco office on the telephone. You think it is too early for the San Francisco office to be open, because it is in a different time zone. You should _____ .

   A. remind your employer of the difference in time between your city and San Francisco, and tell him you will place the call as soon as the office is open

   B. take a chance and call the San Francisco office because someone may be there early

   C. just wait until you think the office will be open, and then place the call

6. You get a personal telephone call while your employer is standing by your desk. You should _____ .

   A. ask the caller if you may return the call later

   B. ask your employer if you may take time out to talk with the caller

   C. try to find out quickly what the caller wants and to make the conversation as brief as possible

7. A long distance call from an important advertiser comes in while your employer is talking on another line with someone in the company. You should _____ .

   A. ask the caller to hold on, and then show the employer a note telling him about the call

   B. tell the advertiser that you will call back as soon as your employer is free

   C. ask the caller to hold on, wait until the other call is finished, and then put him through to your employer

8. A conference is going on in your employer's office. The secretary to one of the people in the meeting calls and says she has a very important message for her boss and must talk with him. You should _____ .

   A. enter the office and tell the person involved

   B. ask the secretary to wait, and give the person a note

   C. switch the call immediately to your employer's office

9. A person calls whose name you do not recognize as that of a regular caller. Your employer is doing some paper work at his desk. You should _____ .

   A. call your employer to the phone immediately

   B. ask the caller if you can take a message and tell him you will call him back when your employer is available

   C. find out what the person is calling about, and ask him to hold on while you ask your employer if he wants to talk with the caller

10. You have a meeting with a client but are expecting a very important call. You should _____.

   A. set your cell phone ring volume to high to ensure you hear any call

   B. turn your cell phone off

   C. tell your client you are expecting a phone call

SECTION 3   PRACTICE

In this section, proper etiquette will be learned through different tasks.

Task 1   Starting a conversation on the phone

Work in groups of three. Student A is a telephone operator, student B is a caller, and student C is the person the caller wants to speak to. Take it in turns to practice the opening sentences of a phone call. Here are some expressions to help you get through.

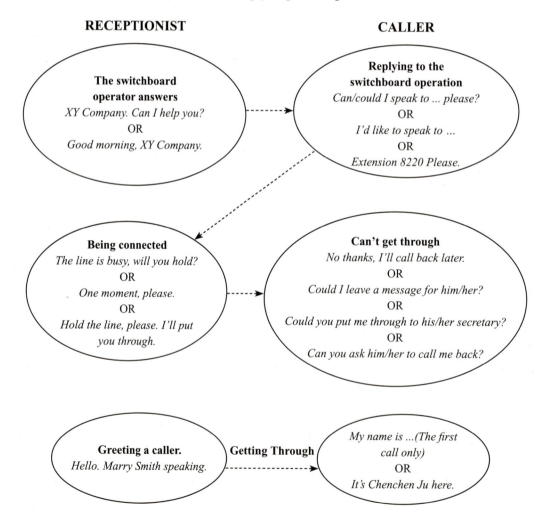

Task 2 Evaluating the conversations

Evaluate the call taker's performance in each of the following telephone conversations, and improve the parts that are handled improperly. Finally role-play them with a partner.

Conversation 1

(*Bill Stalest calls Mr. Walter Brown.*)

Bill Stalest: This is Bill Stalest. May I speak to Walter?

Secretary: Mr. Brown is out of town this week. May I take a message or help you?

Bill Stalest: Perhaps you can help me. Can you give the date of the AMS convention?

Secretary: Yes, I believe I can. Let me check. (You place Mr. Stalest on hold. You return three minutes later with the information only to discover that Mr. Stalest has hung up.)

Conversation 2

(*Mrs. Paul has just stepped out of her office when the telephone rings.*)

Secretary: Good morning, Mrs. Paul's office, Carol Cao speaking.

Caller: Good morning. May I speak to Mrs. Paul?

Secretary: Sorry, she's left the office.

Caller: Oh, how can I contact her?

Secretary: What's the matter?

Caller: Well, nothing's the matter. Thank you.

Conversation 3

(*Ralph McArthur calls Mrs. White.*)

Caller: This is Ralph McArthur. May I speak to Mrs. White?

Secretary: I am sorry, but Mrs. White went over to see Peter Marks of IPP about an advertising matter. She should be back in about two hours. May I have her call you then?

Caller: Yes, please. My number is 86627695.

Secretary: Thank you.

Conversation 4

(*A secretary receives the call from the caller.*)

Ring! Ring! Ring! Ring! Ring! Ring! Ring! Ring! Ring! Ring!

Secretary: Hello.

Caller:	Is this Leask Community School?
Secretary:	Yep.
Caller:	What time is it there?
Secretary:	1:30.
Caller:	May I speak with the principal please?
Secretary:	May I ask who's calling?
Caller:	This is Mr. Ditto from Perfect Copy Systems.
Secretary:	I'm sorry. I don't know where the principal is.
Caller:	The reason I'm calling is to discuss the problems that the personnel department in your school are having with the photocopier. Could you elaborate so that I would have an idea how to solve the problems?
Secretary:	Sorry, it's not my job to know what problems others are having. You'll have to ask the principal but she's still not here.
Caller:	When will she be back?
Secretary:	I don't know.
Caller:	Could I leave a message?
Secretary:	Okay, I'll put you on hold so that I can get a pen.
(*Waits 5 minutes*)	
Secretary:	Okay, what's your name again? And your telephone number?
Caller:	It's Mr. Ditto from Perfect Copy Systems. My number is 212-424-3000.
Secretary:	Okay, I'll leave this message on her desk.
Caller:	Good-bye. (*Click*)
Secretary:	Oh! He hung up!

Task 3 Practicing different phone calls

Work in pairs. Student A is Mr. White's secretary. Student B is a caller. Take it in turns to practice the phone calls in these situations.

Situation 1: The caller tries to get through to the manager, Mr. White, but he is not in the office.

Situation 2: The caller asks something about the company's product. The secretary needs to check some materials, so she/he asks the caller to hold on.

Situation 3: The manager is meeting a visitor. One employee asks the manager to take the call from a person who said he is a friend of the manager.

Situation 4: One client calls angrily because there are some problems with the product he bought.

Task 4 Testing your cell-phone manners

Test your cell phone manners by choosing A, B or C in the following situations and then write a brief report about the result and compare it with your partner.

1. When talking on a wireless phone in public, you _____.
    A. talk loudly because cell phone connections are not that good
    B. get caught up in the conversation and do not realize how loud you are talking
    C. talk in a normal tone because cell phone technology is so good that a whisper could be heard on the other end
2. When entering a movie theater, you _____.
    A. turn your phone off or place it on silent so you will not disturb others in the audience
    B. put your phone on vibrate
    C. keep your phone on its normal ringer, so you do not miss any calls
3. You are in a meeting or a lecture and your phone rings. You _____.
    A. don't worry about it ringing; you have already set the phone on silent
    B. take the call because it is more important than the meeting/lecture you are in
    C. remove yourself from the meeting/lecture to take the call because you have already alerted your colleagues/teacher that you are expecting a call
4. You are dining out with friends at a restaurant and your phone rings. You _____.
    A. apologize and let the call go to voicemail, then turn off the ringer
    B. step outside to take the call because you have already told your friends that you are expecting a call
    C. take the call at the table
5. You're in a restaurant and receive a text message. You _____.
    A. have no problem replying right away
    B. answer after a break in the conversation because texting is less disruptive than making a call
    C. do nothing. Texting is just as rude as making a call

SECTION 4   CASE STUDY

Read the following cases and do each case study in small groups. The questions in "Critical thinking" after each case are aimed to help with finding the story background, the problem itself, the etiquette involved, and the cultural differences behind the etiquette. Remember to provide possible solutions to the problem in each case.

Case 1

June Dally-Watkins Says Sloppy Phone Manners Could Destroy Your Business

Office workers have "appalling" phone manners, and their sloppy skills could destroy your business, says Australia's etiquette queen.

June Dally-Watkins said the way people answered the phone today was shocking, often with just a "yeah," "what" or "speak to me."

"All the yeps, yeahs and uh-huh. I am totally appalled," Ms. Dally-Watkins said.

She said a formal "good morning" or "good afternoon" followed by your name was the only acceptable way to answer the phone, the Herald Sun reports.

She said the informal, rude and abhorrent way young people answered the phone could do severe damage to any business.

"If you are sincere about running a worthwhile business, the very first thing you do is to employ someone on the front desk who not only looks attractive but who answers the phone in the correct and caring way," she said.

Ms. Dally-Watkins, who has been teaching personal deportment for almost 60 years, said a simple "hello" or using first names in business was not acceptable.

"Young people these days are the 'me' generation and are totally involved in themselves," she said.

"They have no right to refer to people by their first name, ever. There is a lack of respect to other people on the other end of the phone. Those values of the past are ones that must be maintained."

However, RMIT University technology lecturer John Lenarcic said the advent of the mobile phone and caller ID had led to shorter, sharper conversations, with little room for niceties: "We are streamlining conversations and removing politeness rituals. You don't need an initiating greeting; you can just jump straight in."

Ms. Dally-Watkins also advised people to avoid asking "How are you?" when they greet someone on the phone.

"I think 'How are you?' is absolutely terrible ... What do people say if they are terribly sick and dying?"

University of Melbourne sociologist Dr. Tim Marjoribanks said the advent of text messaging had left many people unsure how to speak on the phone.

Slade Group recruitment expert Louise Craw said poor-mannered young people with lazy phone skills were very hard to place.

"When people arrive for an interview with a water bottle in their hand and sunglasses on their head, you know times have changed," she said.

Critical thinking

1. Retell the case in 3–4 sentences using the expressions in the box.

yeps and yeahs	appall	informal and rude
correct and caring	"How are you?"	terrible
"hello"	acceptable	shorter and sharper
an initiating greeting	text-messaging	hard to place

2. Read the following statements and relate them to the experts' names correctly. Whose opinion do you agree with more about the initiating greeting on business phone calls?

   A. June Dally-Watkins
   B. John Lenarcic
   C. Tim Marjoribanks
   D. Louise Craw

   (___) In a culture of text-messaging, people tend to be unsure how to speak on the phone.
   (___) The phone conversations are getting shorter and sharper and you don't need an initiating greeting.
   (___) "How are you?" is absolutely terrible when answering a business phone call.
   (___) Young people with poor phone manners are hard to place.
   (___) A simple "hello" or using first names in business was not acceptable.

3. How will you respond when others greet you during a business call with "How are you?" in English? What are the appropriate ways to initiate greetings on phone and to respond to the greetings in a business situation?

Case 2

A Personal Story Why I Dislike People with Bad Telephone Manners

One would think when calling between two professional organizations that one could reasonably expect that the person on the other end of the line would be professional and courteous.

If you call me at work (and sometimes at my home number), you would hear me answer "Professional Business … This is Jaycee Last Name … How can I help you?" However, I don't get that many times when I call other "professionals." Instead I will hear "yes," "what," "hello," etc. Come on now what if I dialed the wrong number? If I assume that you are the person that I was dialing I could give away secure data and then I could get fired. It is also common courtesy if you are the person calling to identify who you are and what company or governmental office you are affiliated with and if you don't I am going to play 20 questions with you before I am going to discuss any pertinent information with you so please save us both a little time and tell me upfront.

I shouldn't have to say this but place your gum in a tissue BEFORE you call me. I don't want to listen to you chewing it like a cow chews cud while I am trying to focus on our conversation.

I don't want to listen to you consume your lunch either so keep that for AFTER we have talked.

When you are talking to me please don't say "ummm ummmm ummmm" over and over in our conversation. This leads me to start counting them and I will lose focus on what you are saying.

Okay I have many more concerns but these are the ones that aggravate me the most.

Critical thinking

1. Retell the case in 3–4 sentences using the expressions in the box.

| professional and courteous | call me at work | assume |
| identify | lose focus on | aggravate |

2. What are the situations that the author was not happy about when making business phone calls? How would you respond when being treated this way?

3. What behaviors are considered as professional when making business phone call? Why are these behaviors important?

SECTION 5   READING FOR ETIQUETTE TIPS

Read the following passages and finish the exercises after each of the texts.

Passage 1

Learn Proper Basic Telephone Etiquette

Telephone is part of us. What would we do without it? It is as common as apple pie and summer sunshine. Therefore, learning proper telephone etiquette is of vital importance. The following are some basic telephone tips.

● Think about what time it is when placing a call. On a work morning before 7:00 a.m. would not be a good time. After 9:00 p.m. in the evening is also not a good time, and remember to avoid calls around the usual period most people will be eating. Calling a business at or very near closing time is to say the least unthoughtful.

● Let the telephone ring a reasonable length of time. It is frustrating to just get to the telephone and hear a dial tone. Answer the phone on the third ring.

● Apologize promptly and hang up, if you dial a wrong number. Dial carefully and in proper lighting to avoid calling a wrong number and inconveniencing others.

● State your name when placing a call. The game of "guess who this is" may not play very well with a busy friend. The proper way to answer the telephone is "hello" or "John Smith speaking." On the other hand, simply answering "yes" is a curt and inappropriate response.

● If you are rushed and can't talk, it's better to say this and make plans to call back later. Don't rustle papers or work while you're speaking on the phone. If you're really too distracted to speak, then reschedule the call.

● Both the caller and receiver should be ready to write down information when required. Before making a call, or taking one, be certain to have a working writing implement, any information one may need to give, and something to write on.

• Keep phone calls brief and friendly. Especially when speaking to anyone who is working and time is of the essence, make your call informative and short.

• Speak softly. Cell phones are usually more sound sensitive than regular phones, so you don't need to yell to make yourself heard, and no amount of shouting will improve a bad connection. Respect the personal space of others by taking your conversation 10 or more feet away from people. Ideally, take your phone call into a private space. Refrain from using your phone in a place where others can't escape your conversation, such as in an elevator or on public transit.

• Do not interrupt a face-to-face conversation to take a cell-phone call. The person you are actually with takes priority. If you have a phone conversation in front of that person, you're showing that he or she is unimportant to you.

• Keep private matters private. Nobody wants to hear you fight with your spouse over your cell phone. If you use the phone for business, you could leak company-confidential information when talking in public.

• Be wary of novelty ring tones. Not everyone will appreciate hearing the latest Britney Spears tune or Beethoven's Fifth every time you receive a call. Try using your phone's "vibrate" function instead of the ringer in public.

• Turn your cell phone off. During weddings, funerals, movies, live performances, sports events, business meetings, classes, and dates, and in places of worship, restrooms, restaurants, libraries, museums, and doctor or dentist waiting rooms, you will turn off your cell phone.

• Focus on driving. While driving, don't make or answer calls. Place calls when your vehicle is not moving, and use a hands-free device to help focus attention on safety. Always make safety a priority.

Exercises

Choose the best answer to each question.

1. When placing phone calls to your friend, _____.
    A. you don't have to state your name first every time
    B. you don't have to wait until 7:00 a.m. on a working day
    C. you don't have to take notes when taking a message
    D. you don't have to return each of his/her phone calls that you missed

2. What's the proper way to answer the telephone in daily life?

   A. "Hello, who are you?"

   B. "Yes?"

   C. "John Smith speaking."

   D. "Guess who?"

3. When using your phone, you need to _____.

   A. speak loudly if the connection is bad

   B. refrain from speaking on your phone in an elevator

   C. walk into a right place to respect your party on phone

   D. speak softly and friendly while speaking to a lady

4. When having a face-to-face conversation with a business acquaintance, you _____.

   A. turn off your cell phone to show respect

   B. answer the phone call in front of him/her

   C. select a novelty ring tone to show your taste

   D. avoid talking about private matters on the phone in front of him/her

5. In which situation should you avoid or stop speaking on the phone?

   A. Crossing a street.

   B. Attending weddings.

   C. Watching performances.

   D. All of the above.

Passage 2

Office Telephone Etiquette

As your company's representative, your phone manners should be **impeccable** (无瑕的，无可挑剔的). A telephone call is frequently the very first contact customers and potential customers have with a company and is the basis for their first impression of that company. The following eight techniques will ensure your business portrays a professional and courteous tone on the telephone.

• Answer all telephone calls promptly. Do you want your customers to feel that they are valuable to your company? Of course you do! In order to do so, all telephone calls should be answered within three rings. By answering telephone calls within three rings, the customer will feel as though their call is important and their needs will be addressed in a timely manner.

• A positive attitude and friendly tone should be used when answering the telephone. If the phone is answered with an unenergetic tone, how do you expect the customer to be enthusiastic about your company? By maintaining a positive attitude and answering the phone with a "smile" in your voice, your customers will feel confident about your company and happy to do business with you.

- Always use appropriate greetings when answering the telephone. Do you want your customers to know what company they have reached when they call? Absolutely! Answering the telephone by clearly and slowly stating the company name and the representative's name will ensure the customer that they have contacted the right organization. Furthermore, the customer will feel more of a "personal touch" when the operator's name is stated at the time the call is answered.

- Listening to the caller is **imperative** (必要的) to ensure their needs are addressed accurately. Everyone wants to be heard, so be sure to listen up! It may also be helpful to keep paper and pens by the phone to jot down notes while the customer is stating the purpose of their call. This ensures the call will be handled and/or directed properly.

- Transferring calls correctly assures the customer that they are being transferred to the correct department or person. Prior to transferring the call, the caller should be told that they will be transferred. Would you want to be blindly transferred to an extension where the phone rings and rings? Of course not! Therefore, as an example, a possible statement to use is "One moment while I transfer you to the Sales Department." It is very disheartening to callers when they are transferred "cold" without any forewarning as it gives them the impression they will be transferred incorrectly.

- In the busy times we are in, placing callers on hold should be handled very carefully. Have you ever been placed on hold without your permission? It definitely does not set a professional tone for the caller. Therefore, when it becomes necessary to place callers on hold, the caller should be asked if they would mind holding prior to doing so. For example, a statement like this can be used, "May I put you on hold for just one moment?" This allows the caller to respond in a positive manner. In addition, if the caller is on hold for more than 30 seconds at a time, checking back with them every 30 seconds is important to assure the customer realizes their call is being addressed. Lastly, once the caller is officially taken off of hold, they should be thanked for waiting. This leaves the caller with a good impression of the company.

- Handling messages is particularly important to assure the caller that their message will be delivered to the appropriate party. When the person or department the caller is trying to reach is unavailable, the caller should be offered the opportunity to leave a voice message in either the voice mail box or via a personal message. As an example, the caller can be asked which they would prefer by simply saying, "The Sales Department is assisting other callers, would you like to leave a voice mail or personal message?" If the caller chooses to leave a personal message, the message should be repeated back to them for accuracy.

• Ending the phone call properly leaves a favorable lasting impression with the caller. Always end the phone call on a positive note by thanking the caller. This leaves the caller with a positive impression of your company and will ensure repeat phone calls and business!

Exercises

Choose the best answer to each question.

1. If you want your customers to feel that they are valuable to your company, _____.
   A. you answer telephone calls after three rings
   B. you answer telephone calls within three rings
   C. you get ready to pick up the telephone right on the first ring
   D. you must say sorry to the customer if you failed to answer on the first ring

2. When answering the telephone in your office, _____.
   A. you speak with a serious voice to show you are taking it seriously
   B. you talk about sports to show you are energetic
   C. you wear a sweet smile while speaking and the caller will be happy to see that
   D. you state the company's name and your name clearly and slowly

3. You can do the following things to make the customer feel welcome apart from _____.
   A. maintaining a positive attitude while speaking
   B. answering the phone with a "smile" in your voice
   C. using intimate greetings to get closer to each other
   D. answering the phone with a friendly tone all the time

4. When you are transferring the call, you _____.
   A. should ask the caller "May I put you on hold for a moment?"
   B. should transfer the caller directly to save time
   C. should tell the caller he/she will be transferred before you do it
   D. should say thanks to the caller when you have transferred them

5. When the person the caller tries to reach is unavailable, what should you do?
   A. You ask the caller to wait on line for a few minutes.
   B. You ask the caller to leave a personal message or a voice mail.
   C. You tell the caller that person's cellphone number and ask him to contact directly.
   D. You ask for the caller's phone number and promise to give it to that person.

Passage 3

The 8 Rules of Smartphone Business Etiquette

From using emoticons to texting late at night, your phone can get you into trouble if you're not careful. Here are a few guidelines to help you properly separate business from pleasure.

Rule No. 1: Be considerate.

Before you initiate a texting or instant messaging session, ask if the person on the other end is available. If the answer is "no," ask when he or she will be free. Likewise, if a business contact sends you a message, and you can't give the conversation your full attention, be honest. Then graciously provide the person with a better time to connect. "Don't go off on a **rant**(叫嚷) on a business matter without asking contacts first if they are free to talk," says Kristen Ruby, founder and CEO of Ruby Media Group, a social media marketing and PR agency. And be patient. "You shouldn't expect the same immediate response you get when texting or IMing with friends or family members. Give people the same response window you would with traditional email correspondence."

Rule No. 2: Remember the concept of "business hours."

Smartphones have officially taken over the planet, eliminating the idea of the 9-to-5 workday and allowing—for better or for worse—bosses and their employees to email, IM, and text from anywhere at any time. With so much access to so many different forms of communication, as a business owner you can easily forget that not everyone works 24/7. "I've definitely been guilty of emailing or text messaging someone back too quickly from my cell phone or trying to schedule a meeting for well after regular office hours," Ruby says. "Not everyone wants to work beyond traditional business hours or on the weekends. It's really not proper etiquette to contact business partners late at night or on weekends, but during the workday and until 7–9 p.m. is usually fine."

Rule No. 3: Only contact the people you talk to regularly.

Emma Moore, interactive director at design and development firm Fundamental, stresses that instant communication feels the most efficient and natural with the clients and business contacts you frequently contact. "If you are with people all week long, emailing and texting become more regular," she says. "There are more opportunities to gather information with co-workers, so communication will happen more frequently." Still, she sees moderation as key. "Each time a text interrupts an important real-life conversation, my respect and willingness to engage with a person who texts me or who stops talking to me in order to answer a message decrease."

Rule No. 4: Put your phone away during face-to-face meetings.

Due to technology, the in-person meeting has become a lost art—but it's still essential. Moore has witnessed inconsiderate texting and emailing and even phone call interruptions firsthand that have caused her not to sign contracts. "During the initial meetings about a possible project, a potential client checked his phone each time it buzzed," she says. "One out of five messages, he would stop our conversation and respond, making it impossible for anyone to concentrate. His smartphone habits helped me know that working with him would probably be a nightmare. Texting is just not acceptable during meetings. However, right after a meeting is fine. If you are waiting for important information related to the meeting via text or email, be transparent about it beforehand. But don't make it a habit."

Rule No. 5: Texts and IMs should be reserved for simple, non-critical topics.
Avoid the temptation to use instant communication as a way to immediately get in touch about an emergency. Real professional emergencies—especially when they involve emotional or controversial topics—require voice-to-voice and often even face-to-face communication. Communications expert and public speaker Lisa B. Marshall says a text message "is a short message, not an email or a meeting. If the message you want to deliver is important or lengthy, you must call, meet in person, or video chat." If the topic you're texting about could result in a complicated discussion, schedule a phone call or at least craft a clear, concise email. Marshall says this rule is especially important for companies that have international clients, because specific words can have very different meanings that get lost in writing.

Rule No. 6: Be wary of abbreviations and emoticons.
Before you go **hog-wild** (完全控制不住的) with **acronyms** (首字母缩略词) and smiley faces, consider who you're texting, emailing, or IMing. In most cases, colloquial abbreviations like "LOL" and any emoticons shouldn't appear in messages to professional contacts, but use your best judgment. "Younger generations—for example, my interns—prefer texting over conversation," Marshall explains. You might be very comfortable with texting. But you have to realize that older clients and business contacts may not use it very often and thus might not know about common abbreviations. When deciding how to engage with people with your smartphone, consider their comfort zone: "When I text a younger person, I use standard abbreviations," Marshall says, "but when I communicate with clients or business contacts closer to my age, I use proper spelling and grammar."

Rule No. 7: Never send sensitive information.
According to Marshall, due to sensitive information—such as files, links, and passwords—being texted freely between younger employees, all her websites were compromised, causing significant downtime. "Recently, all my websites were hacked, complete with red skulls and crossbones." She adds that the failure of an employee to adhere to Rule No. 6 when posting public messages

online caused additional confusion for visitors to her websites. "I asked an intern to take down our main page and put up a brief message explaining we would return when the website was recovered. She posted 'BRB' on the page, and many of my clients were confused by the message, unaware that 'BRB' stood for 'Be Right Back.'"

Rule No. 8: Stay professional.
Even though texts and IM are by nature more casual than other forms of communication, the quality of your instant messages are still reflections of your business and expertise. Make sure to spell check and not write like an over-excited teenager. Marshall says, "I often chat online with listeners of my podcast. In doing so, I've discovered that IM and text message conversation skills are a critical part of relationship building and networking. Turn-taking still exists, as it does in a regular conversation. Be sure to answer questions, but also ask questions so the conversation can move forward. Delivering compliments and constructive criticism gets attention, but it will not build a relationship."

Exercises

Choose the best answer to each question.

1. What should you consider before you initiate a texting session with your business partner?
    A. Is he/she at home at this moment?
    B. Is he/she able to respond to the message immediately?
    C. Is he/she available right now?
    D. Is he/she using traditional email correspondence?
2. Which of the following statements correctly explains "business hours"?
    A. Business people today work 24/7.
    B. Business partners contact during the workday and until 7–9 p.m.
    C. A CEO can schedule a meeting after regular office hours.
    D. A CEO can frequently contact co-workers late at night and on weekends.
3. It is not acceptable during face-to-face meetings to _____.
    A. stop talking to your client in order to answer a message
    B. be transparent about the message you are waiting for and excuse yourself
    C. stop inconsiderate texting and emailing and even phone calls
    D. text right after a meeting with your client
4. As for using acronyms and smiley faces, you have to keep in mind that _____.
    A. "LOL" should only be used among younger generations
    B. only professional contacts prefer using emoticons in their conversation

C. older clients and business contacts may not use them very often and thus might not know about common abbreviations

D. proper spelling and grammar should never be replaced with colloquial abbreviations in communication

5. When using your smartphone, you should _____.

   A. send sensitive information like files, links, and passwords to your best friend only

   B. use standard abbreviations to post public messages online

   C. be aware that your smartphone is due to outsmart you

   D. use spell check and not write like a teenager when texting business partners

SECTION 6   CULTURAL EXPLORATION

In this section, you will learn Chinese etiquette from the cultural perspective.

Task 1   Understanding Chinese etiquette in ancient poems or famous quotes

Read and study the following ancient Chinese poem related to sending messages in English and then find out its original Chinese version. What message is being conveyed in this poem?

Passing by the Northern Mountains

By Wang Wan

Translated by Xu Yuanchong

My boat goes by green mountains high,
And passes through the river blue.
The banks seem wide at the full tide;
A sail with ease hangs in soft breeze.
The sun brings light born of last night;
New spring invades old year which fades.
How can I send word to my friend?
Homing wild geese, fly westward please!

作者_____
译者_____

_____
_____
_____
_____
_____
_____

Task 2 Learning Chinese traditions related to the etiquette of this unit

Read the following introduction to the history of communication in China and identify the major points in the passage. Then pick out some key words or cultural expressions that help you remember and understand the major cultural points.

> Long before telecommunication was even in the world, humanity was obsessed with this central contact—long-distance communication. Some 4,000 years ago, the earlier methods of spreading messages consisted of smoke signals, fires and drumming, very loud drumming, which were used in Africa and Asia. Horns, whistles and flags also found their place in various situations for communication. Although primitive, these approaches persisted for many years relying on a coded language. Certainly there were other cleverer approaches through the centuries. Records can be found in history books, also in literature works, about how the Chinese trained birds and animals to send messages. The carrier pigeons, the tamed wild geese and eagles, and some domesticated animals like horses were all once serving for people as message deliverers. In addition, throughout its long history, China had been built on a reliable and well-running **post house** (驿站) system which supported the long-distance communication around the whole country for thousands of years.
>
> The history of telecommunication is a story of revolution with inventions based on earlier ideas. The use of electricity changed everything since 1820s. Samuel Morse created the telegraph in 1840s. Soon, the wires extended across the countries, even under the ocean. Instant long-distance communication was finally a reality. The telephone, invented in 1876, became a household device in 1940s. The first Email from China to another country was sent in 1987 from Beijing to Karlsruhe University, Germany, which read, "Cross the great wall we can reach each corner of the world." Also in this year, Xu Feng, a young Chinese businessman purchased a cellphone in Guangzhou and selected the first mobile phone number 901088 for himself, thus being the first buyer of a cellular phone in the Chinese mainland. Smartphones emerged in 1990s and text messaging as well as phone calls

Unit 5　Making Telephone Calls

> became one of the major means of communication. In 1998, China had its first independent R&D (research and development) and produced mobile phones created by Kejian Co., Ltd., in Shenzhen, Guangdong. Now in the 21st century, China has become one of the top telecommunication technology R&D centers in the world.

1. Major cultural points in the story:
    (1) _____
    (2) _____
    (3) _____
2. Major words or cultural expressions in the story:
    (1) Para. 1 _____
    (2) Para. 2 _____
3. What interesting stories about communication or telecommunication would you like to share with your classmates?

Unit 6
Interviewing

You will learn in this unit
- ☐ preparing for an interview
- ☐ behaving properly in an interview
- ☐ dressing properly for an interview
- ☐ following up after an interview

SECTION 1 INTRODUCTION

🎧 **Listen to the following passage and fill in the blanks.**

E. T. Hall, an anthropologist, categorizes cultures as high-context or low context. Most Western culture is the low-context culture where 1._____ are highly valued. Employers highly regard 2._____, confidence and being proactive. These qualities are often the determining factors for whether an interview is successful or not.

Candidates are expected to possess high self-esteem and feel confident about "selling" themselves to employers. The tone of the interview is mostly 3._____. Therefore, the interviewees should avoid 4._____ about their own abilities, experience or their background. It is not well received to 5._____ or hesitancy.

Interviewees must also be aware of 6._____ made about areas such as eye contact, tone of voice, attire, gestures, posture, and so on. For example, in most Western countries, eye contact is a sign of 7._____. Similarly, to speak loudly and clearly may be construed to be 8._____ and a firm handshake sends 9._____ confidence and power.

In addition, dressing appropriately according to 10._____ is important because the first judgment an interviewer makes is going to be based on how you look and what you are wearing.

SECTION 2 CHECK YOUR MANNERS

Read the following statements, then mark T for the true statements and F for the false statements. Provide corrections for the false ones.

___ 1. When greeting someone for the first time, a cupped handshake (in which your left hand covers the normal handshake) is a good way to show my sincerity and interest.

___ 2. At an interview or meeting, it is generally necessary for me to stand only when a woman walks into the room (regardless of my gender).

___ 3. I should always turn off (or silence) my cell phone before heading into any interview or business meeting.

___ 4. When on an on-site interview, if I get a parking ticket while at the interview, I can add the cost of the ticket to the expense reimbursement form I submit to the company.

___ 5. After a job interview, regardless of whether I am still interested in the job or not, I should always follow-up with a thank-you letter.

___ 6. A few days after a job interview, I should call the employer every day to see when a hiring decision will be made.

___ 7. When I know a company I am interviewing with is having a casual day on the day I am being interviewed, it is best to dress down for the interview.

___ 8. When talking on the phone with a potential employer or an interviewer, it's okay for me to put them on hold while I answer another phone call.

___ 9. I always avoid asking questions at an interview because it is rude to interrupt the interviewer by asking questions.

___ 10. During an on-site interview, when dining out, I always rest my soup spoon and butter knife on the saucer or plate rather than on the table.

SECTION 3   PRACTICE

In this section, proper etiquette will be learned through different tasks.

Task 1   Preparing for an interview

Good preparation helps to make a successful interviewee. Work in pairs and discuss how to get prepared for an interview. Some key words are provided to help you. Give brief oral reports after your discussion. You may add some other points to the list if possible.

1. Resume and cover letter

_____.

2. The company

_____.

3. Dress code

_____.

4. Punctuality

_____.

5. Questions to ask

_____.

6. Other

_____.

Task 2 Dressing appropriately for an interview

Women's typical interview dress

Men's typical interview dress

Dressing appropriately can make a good impression at a job interview. Follow the three steps below to understand dress code and choose the appropriate dress according to the interview occasion.

Step 1: Research the company's dress code.

Before the interview, you should research the company to have a sense of the workplace and understand what level of formality is appropriate.

The dress code of the company that will be interviewing you could be business professional or business casual. If there is no specific dress code, then choose the business professional.

Step 2: Decode dress code—business professional and business casual.

Study the following pictures and explanations carefully to understand the differences between business casual and business professional.

Business Professional/Formal: the professional standard is to wear a two-piece, matching suit in gray, navy, or black.

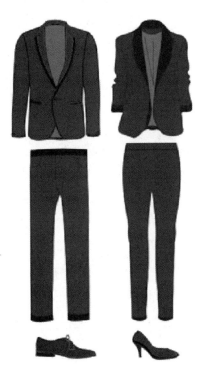

Business Professional is
- matching suit;
- dark colors;
- closed-toe shoe/low heal;
- button down shirt;
- formal blouse.

Business Professional is not
- open-toe shoes;
- khaki pants;
- short sleeve jackets;
- low-cut clothing.

Business Casual: Appropriate business casual dress typically includes **slacks** (便裤) or **khakis** (卡其裤), dress shirt or blouse, open-collar or polo shirt, a dress or skirt at knee-length or below, and **loafers** (休闲鞋) or dress shoes that cover all or most of the foot.

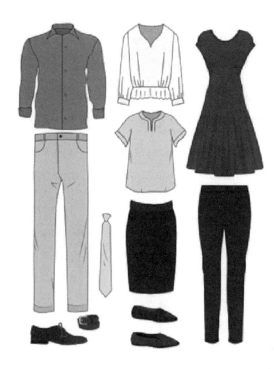

Business Casual is
- **collared** (有圆领的), button down shirts **tucked in** (塞进);
- blouse or shirts with a conservative cut;
- sweaters or **cardigans** (开衫);
- khaki or dark pants with a belt;
- skirts or dresses that fall just above the knees.

Business Casual is not
- **flip flops** (人字拖) or **sandals** (凉鞋);
- gym/athletic attire;
- jeans;
- shorts.

Step 3: Rehearse.

Make a list of items that you should wear or take to the interview. Select them one by one by ticking them of the list. The first one has been done as an example. Try on the dress several days before the interview. Getting accustomed to the dress will help you build your confidence during the interview, and feel less nervous.

Items	Items you should wear or bring		Put a tick here if they are ready
	Men	Women	
Coat			√
Suit or suit skirt	Suit: solid color—navy, black or dark grey	Suit skirt: long enough so you can sit down comfortably	
Shirt or blouse			
Belt			
Tie			
Socks or pantyhose			
Shoes			
Jewelry			

continued

Items	Items you should wear or bring		Put a tick here if they are ready
	Men	Women	
Hairstyle			
Beard			
Nails			
Perfume and make-up			
Portfolio or briefcase			
Cellphone			
ID card			
Gum/breath mint			
Coffee or soda			

Task 3　Meeting the interviewer

Work in pairs, with one student performing the role of an interviewer and the other performing the role of an interviewee. Work together to show how an interview might go smoothly and successfully. Suppose you are in the following situations:

A. Bill is a freshman and looking for a position in the University's Student Union. When at middle school, he played an active role in the school's student union for 3 years. Today, he is meeting the chairperson of the student union …

B. Catherine has passed the entrance examination for Harvard's business school. She's submitted her application, and now she has an interview …

Some questions you may cover:

1. Tell me about yourself.
2. Why do you want to come here to work (for further study)?
3. What aspects of your courses/experience are most relevant to the position?
4. What are your weaknesses?
5. Why do you want to leave your present position?
6. May I ask you some personal questions?

Task 4 Getting ready for the interview

Harry Chan is preparing for a job interview. He is practicing how to conduct himself in the interview. Here is a list of situations. Can you help him to decide what to do in these situations? Three answers are offered in each situation but some of them may be misleading. Please mark the misleading answers with a × and then provide more answers if possible.

Situation	What should you do?
1. Before you have an interview, you should	a. collect the relevant information about the company; b. know how to get there; c. telephone the interviewer to ask how they test the candidates; d. _____.
2. When you go to the interview, you should take your	a. ID card; b. driving license; c. marriage license; d. _____.
3. The appropriate dress for an interview is	a. both men and women in suits; b. men in suits, women in dresses; c. men dress casually, women dress formally; d. _____.
4. When entering the room, you should	a. just say hello to the interviewer; b. smile at the interviewer without saying anything; c. say hello to the interviewer with a smile without reaching out your hand to him/her first; d. _____.
5. If you are asked for the reasons to quit your previous job, you should	a. speak ill of your previous boss and the company; b. speak ill of yourself; c. tell the truth without being malicious; d. _____.
6. During the interview, you can talk about your	a. qualification and experience; b. childhood and friends; c. expected salary and further development; d. _____.
7. When you have received a signal to end the interview, you should	a. rise from your seat, shake hands with the interviewer and say "thank you"; b. rise from your seat, ask when you will get the reply and say "thank you"; c. shake hands with the interviewer while remaining seated; d. _____.
8. After the job interview, you should	a. send a thank-you letter to the interviewer every day until you get a reply; b. send a thank-you letter to the interviewer within 24 hours; c. send a thank-you letter to the interviewer after a few days to ask for a reply; d. _____.

SECTION 4 CASE STUDY

Read the following cases and do each case study in small groups. The questions in "Critical thinking" after each case are aimed to help with finding the story background, the problem itself, the etiquette involved, and the cultural differences behind the etiquette. Remember to provide possible solutions to the problem in each case.

Case 1

My Interview Days

I decided to write this from the view point of the interviewer. Most of us have had awful job interviews but have you ever thought about the person doing the interview?

I was the assistant manager for a large DIY store and one of my roles was carrying out the initial interviews for new staff. This job fell to the assistant manager for good reasons—it was often a case of weeding out candidates who fell far short of our criteria. Only once this process was complete would the store manager himself be involved in the final selection process. The jobs I interviewed for ranged from stock assistant to department managers so I saw a wide range of people.

One gentleman appeared in shorts and a vest—the vest had seen better days. I asked him if he had come straight from work and he replied that no, he hadn't, he just felt relaxed in his shorts and vest.

Another man came and literally gave me his life story before he had got through the door. He had seven children under the age of ten. He lived with his second partner and her three cocker spaniels. He had traveled all over the world but was now looking for a permanent position. He could work any hours we liked apart from Tuesdays, Sundays and Fridays because he had other jobs on those days.

A lady came and muttered something to me as she thrust a letter into my hands. "Sorry, I did not catch that," I said. "Mutter, mutter" again, I did not understand so I looked at the letter. It said: "This is my friend Karina. She does not speak any English but would like to work for your store as she enjoys plants—the garden center is her first choice, or the tool section. I recommend her heartily as she is very kind and good with people. Please give her the job and let me know how she gets on." There was a telephone number and address at the bottom of the letter.

Another young man came in. Initially, he seemed fine. He had a lot of qualifications, some of which were really impressive. He had eight GCSEs with good grades, 3 A levels with A, B and C grades, a diploma in manufacturing and a first aid certificate. I asked him where he went to school and he said, "Oh, several. I took the GCSEs early and went up a year to take my A levels."

I asked him where he had done his diploma—he replied that he could not quite remember only it was a local college. I asked him if he really had all those qualifications. He said no! I asked him why he put them on his form. He said he would never have got the interview otherwise. How true!

Another lady told me she had actually worked at another branch of our store in Manchester. I asked her who the manager was and she told me. I asked her if she left because she had moved away and she said, "Yes, we moved to London so I had to leave."

She knew the store's staff criteria inside out and gave a really good interview. I told her she would hear from us shortly.

On a whim I called the manager in Manchester—turned out she had left but not only because she moved away. She and her family had stolen a lot of goods from the store and other places and were wanted by the police in Manchester. I decided not to call her back.

Another man glanced at my business card that I gave him, and placed it face-down on the table. Perhaps he didn't want to be distracted by reading my card I thought? Every time I asked the candidate a question, he looked at me for a second as he started his answer and then shifted his eye-contact and body language towards my male colleague—it remained there throughout the whole answer. I began to feel that if he could put up a screen between us and conducted the interview solely with my colleague, he would.

I was unsurprised to find that he left my business card on the table when the interview was over. Had I been a sensitive soul, I might be in therapy as we spoke.

Another man decided the way to get the job was to flirt. He sat really close, almost hugging the desk opposite me. He kept asking me if I was married, if I had children, and if there was a chance of a drink after the interview.

Amongst these "reprobates" there were many good candidates and we managed to fill our staff quota plus have some on the waiting list but it never failed to amaze me how some people thought they could walk into a job with a whole load of rubbish on their forms or carry out such poor interviews.

Looking back I suppose it was either funny or sad, depending how you look at it but I know one thing—I dreaded interview days!

Unit 6 Interviewing

Critical thinking

1. Retell the case in 3–4 sentences using the expressions in the box.

assistant manager	in shorts and a vest	life story
mutter	diploma	steal
business card	eye-contact	flirt

2. What did the interviewer in this case think of each candidate and why did she dread interview days? If you were the interviewer, how would you evaluate each candidate's performance?

3. What etiquette rules should a candidate pay attention to when having an interview? Please list at least three of the rules you have learned from the case.

Case 2

What Can Happen When You Are Not Prepared

I remember my first job interview.

I was lucky—I didn't even have to apply for the job.

A friend of mine had a marketing position for a small web design company in downtown Montreal (Canada) and they were looking to add someone just like him to their team. I didn't have much marketing experience but this was a junior position and as a Computer Science major, I had spent more time online than pretty much anyone else I knew.

My friend was able to get me the interview invite simply by mentioning to his boss that yes, he did actually know someone who might be a good fit. One phone call later and I was all set with a date and time bright and early in the morning a few days later.

I did no homework for the interview.

If I knew the name of the company, it was because my friend had mentioned it. I certainly didn't visit their website or check for press mentions, and LinkedIn hadn't been invented yet or I would have ignored that too.

I vaguely remember forwarding my resume to my friend before the interview, but his boss probably didn't read it before we started. Or even need to, because there wasn't much there to read.

I had no clue.

On the day of the interview, I was a little early to the company offices and arrived with a paper copy of my resume in hand. I'd slept well, was well-dressed, feeling good and happy to see that my friend was already there too, as he opened the door to let me in. His boss invited both of us to sit down in their front office lounge, offered a drink (which I refused), and we got underway.

The boss quickly scanned my resume and asked some quick questions to basically confirm what I'd listed there. Maybe he sensed that I was nervous and just wanted to break the ice, but I remember feeling confident.

And then everything went downhill quickly.

"It says here that you speak French fluently, is that correct?"

"Yes, that's right," I replied.

"What's the French word for 'browser'?"

I had no clue.

I frantically searched my mind, but if there was a French word for "browser," I hadn't heard it.

I was supposedly bilingual and supposedly very familiar with Internet terminology, so if there was a French word for "browser," I should have heard it.

I really had no clue.

"I … I don't know," I stammered, and my face said it all. It felt like I had been caught in a lie, which I had been, frankly.

And just like that, it was over.

There may have been another language-related question that I didn't know, but the boss had heard what he needed to and was very curt about it. He said something like "I think we'll stop here. Good luck with your job search." He didn't thank me for coming in, but he also didn't thank me for wasting his time either. After the fact, I felt bad that perhaps my poor interview would lessen the boss's esteem for my friend and cause him problems at work, but if it ever happened, my friend never said anything.

What could I have done better?

I could have recognized that I wasn't qualified for the job and been clearer with my friend when he asked me about it.

I could have researched what kinds of projects the company was working on, and what kinds of projects the company would need to hire me to work on. LinkedIn didn't exist yet, but I did have a friend on the inside, after all.

I could have been more honest on my resume about my language skills, or at least tried to get someone else's assessment of them, to confirm or reject what I thought I knew before having it done in real time, to my face, embarrassingly in the middle of the interview.

I had no clue.

Critical thinking

1. Retell the case in 3–4 sentences using the expressions in the box.

friend	marketing position	homework	resume
quick questions	downhill	French	done better

2. What mistakes did this candidate make when preparing for this interview? What are the reasons for each of these mistakes respectively?

3. What do you think is the most important element except for dressing properly for the interview? What can you learn from the outcome of this interview?

SECTION 5 READING FOR ETIQUETTE TIPS

Read the following passages and finish the exercises after each of the texts.

Passage 1

How to Stand Out in a Job Interview?

Have you heard the phrase, "The cream rises to the top?" Do you love **root beer** (根啤，根汁汽水) floats, or drinks that are composed of ice cream on top of root beer? You can be "the cream that rises to the top" in your job search by doing things that will set you apart from others who are looking for work.

• The first thing you must do before you have an interview is to display professionalism. Fill out a job application neatly and completely. Follow all the instructions of an ad you are replying to. If you are replying by mail, use resume paper and a resume envelope. Do not provide an email address on your cover letter or resume that is silly or **weird** (古怪的).

● Make your cover letter stand out. To make your letter easy to read, use a font size of at least twelve points. The top left corner should reveal your full address, email address, telephone number and the current date. After you type in this information, hit "Enter" four times and type in the name and address of the company you are sending your letter to.

● Do not say "I" in your cover letter. A good way to avoid using "I" is to start the body of your cover letter with a header that says, "Subject: Response to your ad for the Sales Clerk position you posted on Sunday."

● Put great care into how you address the reader. It is not a good idea to write, "To whom it may concern." If you know the name of the person who will read your letter, address the person by his or her name. If the person's name is Jane Doe, address her as "Ms. Doe." If you do not know the contact's name, you should write, "Dear Sir or Madam."

● The next part of your cover letter should include a bulleted list of your accomplishments, background and skills. Do not supply a long list. I recommend you list up to five good skills and accomplishments that are relevant to the position you are applying for.

● After you list your accomplishments and skills, close your letter by writing, "My resume is enclosed. Thank you for your consideration." Sign the letter in black or blue ink and place your written signature above your typed signature. Read your cover letter twice or more to eliminate any errors.

● Like your cover letter, your resume should be easy to read, look professional and exclude "I." Never use more than two pages for your resume. Include all the jobs and voluntary activities you have done for the past seven years. Provide your job titles, the dates you worked and the names of the companies you worked for.

● Your resume must discuss results you have achieved for your employers. If you are improving your company's bottom line and you have a measurable amount, you could write, "Improving the company's total amount of sales by twenty percent."

● We will now discuss what to do during and after a job interview. Are you familiar with the phrase, "A good first impression is a lasting impression"? You must do several things very well that will create a great image that will stick in the interviewer's mind forever and sway him or her to hire you first.

● Arrive on time, perhaps five to ten minutes early—take a trip to the place of your interview at least one day early to make sure you can find the place. If you are a guy, wear dress shoes, a tie, dress pants and a suit jacket that does not have a loud color such as red, pink, purple, orange or yellow. If you are a lady, wear dress shoes and a suit or dress. Treat the receptionist with respect. Do not arrive with a tobacco smell or bad body odor. Always dress for success. Overdressing is better than dressing too casual. This means dressing as if you were on display, (which you are), even if the company has a reputation for being casual. This will give you the air of one who cares about his appearance and the job you are seeking. Once you've actually got the job, then you can dress as casually as your co-workers.

• Give the interviewer a firm handshake, warm smile and frequent eye contact. Answer questions fully and truthfully. Do not do anything stupid such as eating. Let the interviewer do most of the talking. Do not bring up your personal life or ask about the salary for the position.

• Display a good attitude and good manners. Express a willingness to work a flexible schedule and a willingness to work extra hours when it is necessary. Show interest in the position by asking when you can start. Never attend an interview without doing research on the company, no matter what type of company it is. When I interviewed for a teaching assistant position, I was asked what I knew about the school district. Keep your answers short and to the point, without being **abrupt** (鲁莽的). Practice with a friend in advance of the interview and time your answers to common questions. Practice being relaxed and confident as you answer.

• Always be positive. This means not only being positive about the company and the available position, but also about your former jobs. If you tell the interviewer that your last boss "had it in for you," or that you worked with "a bunch of jerks," you will automatically be eliminated from his list of prospects.

• Thank the interviewer for the interview and ask for his or her business card at the end of the interview. Send a thank-you letter that **reiterates** (重申) your interest and qualifications. Call within a week to find out where you stand in the hiring process. Do everything you have learned to stand out from the other job applicants!

Exercises

Choose the best answer to each question.

1. Which one shows a job applicant's unprofessionalism before the interview?
    A. Filling out a job application neatly and completely.
    B. Following all the instructions of an ad you are replying to.
    C. Using resume paper and a resume envelope when replying by mail.
    D. Providing a silly-but-funny email address on the cover letter to make it stand out.

2. What is true about the cover letter?
   A. Put the job applicant's address and the current date on the bottom of the letter.
   B. Address the reader as "To whom it may concern" whether their name is known or not.
   C. The list of accomplishments should be as long as possible.
   D. The written signature is above the typed signature.
3. What will help interviewees leave a good first impression on the interviewers?
   A. Arrive 5–10 minutes early.
   B. Dress formally.
   C. Show up with no bad odor.
   D. All of the above.
4. What should interviewees do during the interview?
   A. Give the interviewer a firm handshake.
   B. Avoid frequent eye contact with the interviewer.
   C. Lead the conversation most of the time.
   D. Ask about the salary for the position when the interview starts.
5. How should interviewees show their positive attitude?
   A. Talk about your weak points without being asked.
   B. Badmouth the last employer.
   C. Show your interest in the current job.
   D. All of the above.

Passage 2

Things You Should Never Do during and after a Job Interview

The interview is the toughest part of the job application process—it can be nerve-wracking and intense, and it's often difficult to prepare for. Mistakes are easy to make when you're nervous, and the unfortunate truth is that sometimes one mistake is enough to take you out of the running.

During the interview

On the day of the interview, try to avoid these common interview mistakes.

• Poor hygiene and personal appearance. It should go without saying that you should always have good hygiene in a professional environment. No employee wants a smelly co-worker, and recruiters feel the same. Make sure you are clean, polished-looking, and dressed appropriately for the position you are applying for. If you are unsure, err on the side of professional dress more than casual.

• Showing up late. Being late to a job interview isn't just poor manners—it tells the recruiter that you don't care about the job, have more important things to do or just aren't responsible enough to be where you need to on time.

Keep in mind that it can also be rude to show up too early. If possible, wait in a separate area until five minutes before your interview time, then announce yourself to the receptionist or a staff member.

• Being rude to the receptionist or support staff. It is vital that you are kind to everyone in the office when you go in for an interview. You never know who has a say in whether you get the job. Be courteous, professional and polite to everyone you interact with during the entire process, and make sure to thank people for their time as you leave.

• Being too comfortable with the interviewer. You might hit it off with the hiring manager, but you should try to remain professional through the entire hiring process. This goes for social media as well. While it's a great tool for marketing or showing your personality, it's not good for socializing with your potential hiring manager. You also should not attempt to befriend an interviewer on social media. General company accounts are fine, but do not hunt down interviewers' personal accounts.

• Poor body language. Too firm a handshake—crushing hands is no way to win favor. Hand gestures during the conversation are fine, but refrain from fidgeting, such as shaking your leg, tapping your fingers or playing with a pencil. Staring might make an interviewer uncomfortable, but looking the speaker in the eye, with slight breaks to look away, is polite. Frequently looking away or over their shoulder while talking to them conveys disinterest.

• Overseeing what you post on social media. It should be a rule of thumb to avoid crude, offensive or sensitive posts about your interviewing process during your job search. Better yet, remain professional on social media at all times, not just while you're applying for jobs. A professional and polished online presence is important regardless of your career stage.

After the interview
At the end of the interview, you should ask the hiring manager when you can expect to hear back and when it's appropriate to reach out if you haven't heard from them. It is good etiquette to send a thank-you letter to whoever interviewed you within one or two days after the interview and wait for them to respond with next steps. After that, try to be patient and avoid these common post-interview mistakes.

• Too much follow-up. It's all right (and even expected) to follow up after the interview, but don't overwhelm your potential employer with multiple messages and phone calls. If you reach out too often, you're going to turn off the hiring manager.

• No follow-up. After the interview, it is vital to send some form of correspondence—whether it be snail mail, email or even a phone call—thanking your interviewer for their time and effort. Interview follow-up is another opportunity to sell yourself to the interviewer by restating your interest and showing good manners.

• A generic follow-up letter. Most hiring managers can spot a generic thank-you letter (or cover letter, for that matter) a mile away, so take the time and effort to tailor your letter to the interviewer. Bring up something you discussed that isn't strictly related to your skills or the job description.

• Ghosting the company. If you decide the position is not right for you, for whatever reason, be sure to reach out to the company and let them know that you want to withdraw your candidacy. Whoever interviewed you took time out of their busy schedule for you, so the courteous thing to do is to acknowledge that effort with a gracious thank-you and official withdrawal.

• Burning bridges. No matter what happens after the interview, don't burn bridges. If you don't get the particular position, you always send a gracious follow-up to the hiring managers and/or the HR person expressing interest in future opportunities. It will make a good impression and could get you considered for other opportunities.

Exercises

Choose the best answer to each question.

1. During the interview, an interviewee is advised to _____.
    A. have good hygiene
    B. show up very early to a job interview
    C. pay no attention to the receptionist or support staff
    D. hunt down interviewers' personal accounts

2. As an interviewee, which of the following should you pay attention to?
    A. Personal appearance.
    B. Time awareness.
    C. Body language.
    D. All of the above.

3. As an interviewee, which of the following statements is true?
    A. You should try to socialize with your potential hiring manager.
    B. You should look the interviewer in the eye during the whole interview process.
    C. You should avoid shaking your leg or tapping your fingers.
    D. You should post what happened during your interviewing process on social media right away.

4. After the interview, _____ is /are proper.
    A. multiple messages and calls
    B. no follow-up

C. a generic follow-up letter

D. a well-tailored relevant letter

5. After an interview, what should you do as an interviewee?

   A. You should contact the interviewers often to please them.

   B. You should burn bridges if you don't get the particular position.

   C. If you've decided the position is not right for you, you should inform the company.

   D. You should send some form of correspondence to the interviewer, but never make a phone call.

SECTION 6 CULTURAL EXPLORATION

In this section, you will learn Chinese etiquette from the cultural perspective.

Task 1 Understanding Chinese etiquette in ancient poems or famous quotes

Read and study the following six pairs of opposite idioms of four Chinese words about different interview techniques and then find out their original Chinese versions. What messages are being conveyed in these idioms?

1. seek for the virtuous like a thirsty person for water/be jealous of the good and envious of the strong

   _____

2. weigh every word and every sentence with great care/present high-sounding but meaningless talk or writing

   _____

3. answer as quickly as the flowing of water/hesitate in speaking

   _____

4. neither to humble oneself nor to show disrespect/to one's eyes there is no other

   _____

5. be dressed like a gentleman/be careless about one's dress

   _____

6. lay up against a rainy day/stand on the edge of a pool and idly long for fish

   _____

Task 2 Learning Chinese traditions related to the etiquette of this unit

Read the short introduction to two stories about Chinese talent selection and the meanings behind them. Please identify the major cultural points included in the passage, and then pick out some key words or cultural expressions that help you remember and understand the major points.

China has a rich history of talent selection and recruitment. Two important stories, "Three Visits to the Thatched Cottage" and "Mao Sui Recommends Himself," reveal two major characteristics of talent selection in ancient China: the active pursuit of talent and self-recommendation.

"Three Visits to the Thatched Cottage" is the story of Liu Bei visiting Zhuge Liang during the late Eastern Han Dynasty. Liu Bei visited Zhuge Liang three times, inviting him to support Liu-Han governors. Through these three visits, Liu Bei expressed his trust and respect for Zhuge Liang, ultimately winning Zhuge Liang's support. Consequently, Zhuge Liang became Liu Bei's trusted assistant, aiding him in uniting with Sun Quan, capturing Jingzhou and Yizhou, and establishing the Shu-Han regime. "Three Visits to the Thatched Cottage" is celebrated as a beautiful tale, showcasing the leaders' need for and appreciation of talent. They provided opportunities and platforms for truly exceptional individuals, fully harnessing their skills and wisdom to foster the development and progress of the nation.

"Mao Sui Recommends Himself" recounts the story of Mao Sui during the Warring States period. When the Qin army attacked the state of Zhao, the King of Zhao ordered Pingyuan Jun to seek assistance from the state of Chu. Mao Sui, a retainer of Pingyuan Jun, volunteered to accompany him. Following unsuccessful negotiations between Pingyuan Jun and the King of Chu, Mao Sui entered the palace armed with a sword, elucidating the interests at stake, and eventually persuaded the King of Chu to join forces and resist the Qin state's aggression. Mao Sui's self-recommendation exemplifies the proactive self-promotion of talent in ancient China's talent-selection process. The widespread dissemination of Mao Sui's act underscores the courage and initiative of ancient Chinese talents.

These two stories reflect the historical significance of talent selection and recruitment in ancient China and highlight the emphasis placed on recognizing and nurturing exceptional individuals for the benefit of the nation.

1. Major cultural points in the story:
    (1) _____
    (2) _____
    (3) _____
2. Major words or cultural expressions in the story:
    (1) Para. 1 _____
    (2) Para. 2 _____
    (3) Para. 3 _____
3. What interesting stories about talent selection would you like to share with your classmates?

Unit 7
Working at the Office

You will learn in this unit
- ☐ basic concepts of office etiquette
- ☐ creating a professional image
- ☐ behaving properly at the office
- ☐ maintaining positive office relationships

SECTION 1 INTRODUCTION

🔊 **Listen to the following passage and fill in the blanks.**

In the West, management hierarchies tend to be 1._____. As a result, staff in a Western workplace can share their opinions freely. They 2._____ talking to their manager, and they can even call their managers by their first name. The 3._____ communication style is prevalent in Western workplaces. Meanwhile, 4._____ are highly emphasized. Western people place great value on sharing ideas, working together, and promoting a 5._____.

In a Western workplace, 6._____ is usually the main priority. Western people have a strong 7._____. They attach great importance to 8._____, managing time effectively, meeting deadlines, and respecting others' time. Western people tend to prefer formal meetings in which to engage in business activities and it's fairly common for employees to avoid 9._____ with each other. They respect their coworkers' space and keep 10._____ to a minimum.

SECTION 2 CHECK YOUR MANNERS

Choose the best answer for each of the following statements.

1. A colleague begins to tell you a story he heard about a co-worker's private life, so you _____.
    A. diplomatically tell him you're not interested in hearing about it
    B. listen carefully—the more you know about your co-workers, the better equipped you'll be to navigate office politics
    C. listen intently and then rush off to tell someone else in the office all the juicy details

2. A client has been waiting for about five minutes to meet with you but you're running a little behind schedule, and you need a few more minutes to finish up, so you _____.
    A. take a minute to walk out of the office and apologize in person and offer him a cup of coffee and a magazine
    B. have your assistant tell him you are running behind schedule and you will be a few more minutes late
    C. finish what you're working on—you'll get it done faster that way and they'll only have to wait a few more minutes

3. You're charged with the job of collecting money from your coworkers for a colleague's baby shower/birthday present/going-away gift, so you _____.
   A. send a group email, letting people know that you're the designated collector
   B. tell people there's a box in your office into which they can slip their contributions
   C. go door to door
4. You enter a co-worker's office or cubicle to chat and she's on the phone, so you _____.
   A. leave a note saying you need to speak with her and try to get her at another time
   B. stand in the doorway and wait for her to get off—it'll save you the time of having to come back later when she'll probably just be on another call
   C. insist that she speak with you immediately—it's important and you don't have time to wait around
5. You witness one of your co-workers tell the new intern that she "looks really sexy in the short skirts she always wears," so you _____.
   A. privately point out that his comments were sexist and offensive
   B. publicly criticize his character—he needs to be deterred from making similar comments in the future
   C. laugh heartily and voice your agreement—it's just harmless fun
6. You work in an office where casual-dress is the norm and you have a meeting at your company's bank, so you _____.
   A. dust off your best suit—you want to leave nothing to chance
   B. dress up a little more than usual, maybe add a jacket to your ensemble
   C. dress as casually as usual—what counts is the substance of the meeting, not your appearance
7. As the marketing manager in your company you vastly underestimate the time required for your division to complete a project and you come out way over budget, so you _____.
   A. accept responsibility for the error and admit to your staff that you made a mistake and set about to correct it
   B. say nothing, but take action to correct your mistake
   C. attempt to deflect your responsibility for the error by spreading blame around—after all, you can't be perceived as the one who screwed up
8. Your boss calls you into her office to go over your latest report, and she criticizes a significant portion of your work, so you _____.
   A. listen carefully and take time to think about everything she said before offering a response
   B. respond to each criticism as it comes up to insure you don't miss the opportunity to downplay each one
   C. get angry at her and quickly point out many of her shortcomings—she needs to know she's not perfect either and next time maybe she'll think twice before criticizing your work

9. You want a raise and in order to justify it you tell your boss _____.

   A. what new responsibilities you can assume and what you can achieve with the added responsibilities

   B. that your salary is below average for your position in your region

   C. about how expensive your grandfather's nursing home bills are

SECTION 3 PRACTICE

In this section, proper etiquette will be learned through different tasks.

Task 1 Evaluating office etiquette

Work in groups of three or four. First decide whether these behaviors are acceptable or not in an office, and then rank them according to their importance. Finally, analyze and compare your decisions together.

1. Talking loudly on the cell phone
2. Dating colleagues
3. Using the Internet for a private matter
4. Taking credit for co-workers' contribution to a project
5. Coming to work tired and looking sloppy
6. Sharing everything with co-workers
7. Talking to your co-workers about religion and politics
8. Telling your co-workers dirty jokes
9. Sending funny but useless emails to co-workers
10. Chewing gum loudly
11. Not taking one's own responsibility
12. Talking down to co-workers
13. Interrupting co-workers for small talk

Task 2 Communicating with colleagues

How would you react in the following situations and communicate well with your colleagues?

1. After sitting in an office meeting for about 10 minutes, you realize that you don't have much to contribute to the discussion. How do you ask to leave in a professional way?
2. You are in an open office and someone is talking loudly on his mobile phone during a personal call.
3. You need to convey bad news to a colleague. Do you call or email?

4. There is back-stabbing happening in the office and you are encouraged to participate.

5. A co-worker has not submitted a high quality proposal to a client.

6. You offered your colleague John a ride to the lunch, but you forgot about it.

Task 3 Acting as the mediator between the boss and the employees

An employer shares about the problem with his employees. Suppose you are an office etiquette expert, how would you help the employer solve the problem?

> I employ 5 people in a small manufacturing shop. I don't have a problem with my employees talking to each other during work and I also allow them to listen to the radio using earbuds. An issue has come up with my employees regarding my handling of their personal office conversation. Every so often I have a question or instruction for an employee that actually has to do with work. If I walk into the room and determine that the employees are engaged in chattering about personal issues (movies, TV, dates, etc.) I will interrupt the conversation. I will ask the question I have about work or whatever I need to have done. I never have a problem with them talking on work time, but I feel that time is mine and when I need them for work issues everything else should stop for that. The employees on the other hand feel that I should wait until their personal conversation is over before I speak to them about anything. I have felt that I was very lenient about the chatter and that I have the right to interject the issue at hand into the moment. So—am I being rude? Or should I change the rules and allow no conversation? I think that I have been overly generous with the rules, but it shouldn't cause my company to come to a halt because of personal conversations. Please let me know if I need to change my attitude or should they?

SECTION 4 CASE STUDY

Read the following cases and do each case study in small groups. The questions in "Critical thinking" after each case are aimed to help with finding the story background, the problem itself, the etiquette involved, and the cultural differences behind the etiquette. Remember to provide possible solutions to the problem in each case.

Case 1

Working in a Cubicle

Harry usually worked together with his colleagues in New York in a big office where a lot of cubicles were available for the staff. That's OK to work in a cubicle for him. But after Harry began to work with his new colleagues in a cubicle in a big city in another country this year, he complained several times about their behaviors, "my new neighbor was on his phone constantly since he took his seat this morning, and he spoke so loudly that I couldn't concentrate on my work at all."

Now, Harry is talking with Amy about another annoying issue. "You know what, that guy came to my cubicle just now when I was on the phone. He stood next to me smiling and listened to me speaking until I finished the phone call. Then he told me he just wanted to ask a question about our business and he didn't mind having had to wait. What should I do if this happens again?" At that moment, he hears a strange sound. "What is that? Is someone munching on an apple?" Harry asks. "I think my neighbor is munching on potato chips." Amy says …

Critical thinking

1. Retell the case in 3–4 sentences using the expressions in the box.

cubicles	neighbor	phone calls	stood by	strange sound

2. Why did Harry complain? Do his complaints show that he was making a fuss about that?

3. What may be the different interpretations of privacy and personal boundaries in an open office environment in different cultures? If you were Harry, what would you do in those situations? If you were the leader of this office, what would you do to solve this problem?

Case 2

Interpreting a Smile

Peter is the general manager of an American company abroad. Recently, Tom, one of the local managers made a mistake at work that caused some difficulties that required a lot of effort to fix. Tom was very upset about what had happened, and came to Peter's office to make a formal apology.

Tom went into Peter's office after being told to. Smiling before he spoke, "Peter, I've been feeling very upset about the trouble I've caused for the company. I'm here to apologize for my mistake. I'm terribly sorry about it and I want you to know that it will never happen again." Tom said, looking at Peter with the smile he had been wearing since he walked into the office.

Peter found it hard to accept the apology. He looked at Tom, and asked, "Are you sure?"

"Yes, I'm very sorry and I promise this won't happen again," Tom said, with a smile even broader than before.

"I'm sorry I just can't take your apology. You don't look sorry at all!" Peter said angrily. Tom's face turned very red. He had not in the least expected Peter to take it negatively. He was desperate to make himself understood. "Peter," he managed to smile again, "trust me. No one can feel any more sorry than I do about it."

Peter was almost furious by now, "If you're that sorry, how can you still smile?"

Critical thinking

1. Retell the case in 3–4 sentences using the expressions in the box.

| mistake | a formal apology | smile | furious |

2. Why did Tom wear a smile when he made the apology? Do you think it is reasonable that Peter became so angry at Tom? Why or why not?

3. What are the different interpretations of a smile by the two in this situation? If you were Tom, what would you say or do next to make yourself understood?

Case 3

Expressing Different Ideas

David is from Asia and works in a joint-venture as an executive in America. His boss is a Westerner named Steve. They are good friends. Once, at a meeting with mostly Asian participants including David, Steve asked for suggestions on his new project. David and other participants did not express any different ideas so Steve took it for granted that his new project would be quite satisfactory to everyone present at the meeting and decided to implement the plan. But to his surprise and puzzlement, after the meeting, David came to his office and told him that there were problems with the project, and the project might not work properly. This time, to David' surprise, Steve didn't seem happy but even annoyed with this.

Critical thinking

1. Retell the case in 3–4 sentences using the expressions in the box.

| friends | meeting | no different ideas | office | problems | annoyed |

2. Why was Steve not happy? How should David express his opinion to his boss in a Western work environment?

3. Why do people from some cultures prefer giving different opinions privately?

SECTION 5 READING FOR ETIQUETTE TIPS

Read the following passages and finish the exercises after each of the texts.

Passage 1

Basic Workplace Etiquette You Must Follow

Work etiquette is a standard that controls social behavior expectations in the workplace. It covers a wide range of aspects among employees. Some of these include body language, behavior, technology use, and communication. There is no universal agreement to standard workplace etiquette. However, specific proper workplace etiquette rules apply to almost every business.

Pay attention to your appearance

In modern workplaces, appearance is often combined with performance, and it plays a crucial role in business success. If you show up to work every day with a wrinkled shirt, uncombed hair or dirty fingernails, it will be noticed. Whom do you think your supervisor is going to choose to represent the company on a business trip or in a meeting? The person wearing sneakers and T-shirt, or a co-worker who always shows up for work well-groomed and wearing freshly ironed clothes?

Follow the dress code strictly. If the company does not have a dress code, remember that it's better to overdress than underdress. Avoid wearing fancy or too many accessories.

It's great to practice good hygiene, but not so great to do it in public. Save the flossing, hair brushing and eyebrow plucking for the rest room during your lunch hour.

Know how to greet people properly

There's a saying, "You never get a second chance to make a good first impression." Nowhere is this more true than in the office. When meeting people for the first time, it's good practice to make eye contact and give a firm handshake and tell the other person how nice it is to meet him or her. If you already know the person, but others you are with don't, it's necessary to make the proper introductions.

Be there when you're supposed to be
Show up on time and stay until finishing time. If you've ever called a business five minutes before closing and spoken to an employee who'd already mentally gone home, you know what this is about. Stay on the job until it's time to leave.

Know when it's your treat
Lunch meetings help you to get to know a colleague or team better. The rule of thumb is that if you are inviting others for a business lunch, it is your treat. That is, the person offering the invitation should be footing the bill. Make no fuss about it.

Don't leave a messy desk
Business associates will not regard you in a favorable light due to the untidiness of your workspace. No one likes to wait while a co-worker attempts to unearth a missing item from under a mound of papers.

Stay out of office politics
Usually in an office there are one or two "squeaky wheels." These people try to stir things up by complaining, gossiping, or whining. Sometimes the squeaky wheel gets oiled, as the saying goes, but it's certainly not the best way to attract supervisory attention. Try to avoid being around these employees, and don't become one. And it's usually not a good idea to share personal or job-related problems with co-workers. They may only spread rumors and feed the gossip mill that may come back to haunt you.

Maintain virtual office etiquette
Virtual meetings have become a part of our daily work routine. It is a whole different story compared to in-person meetings. Here are six simple points that you need to follow to maintain the perfect virtual workplace etiquette.

• Take a few minutes to get appropriately dressed and brush your hair before starting your day. That's the first step to be productive while working remotely.

• When you join a virtual team meeting, speak up when you are asked to. Do not keep silent, but make sure not to interrupt when someone else is talking.

• Use attentive body language if you're using your webcam. Sit up straight, don't make weird gestures, and don't let your eyes wander too far.

• Mute your microphone when you are not talking as it will help avoid noises.

• Make sure your work setup is professional. A messy room, a screaming child or a barking dog can be distracting.

• Make proper eye contact by looking at the camera.

Other things to take into consideration

• Accept criticism graciously. Try to avoid taking it personally, and use it to improve your performance.

• Avoid the use of **profanity** (亵渎语言). Not only does it make you look bad; it makes others uncomfortable as well.

• Keep your private life out of the workplace as much as possible. Obviously you can't do this every minute, but it's still better to keep outside interference to a minimum.

• Don't borrow money. It can lead to a very uncomfortable situation.

• Don't **slouch** (无精打采). It's a poor reflection of yourself if you're slumped over your desk all day. If you're prone to nodding off during business meetings or at your desk, bring in some coffee to help you stay awake.

• Be careful of an office romance. The impact of dating a co-worker could affect your career and many companies try to ban dating among their employees.

Exercises

Choose the best answer to each question.

1. In modern workplaces, paying attention to your appearance means that you _____.
    A. work every day in casual dress
    B. wear fancy or too many accessories
    C. follow the dress code of the company strictly
    D. practice good hygiene in public
2. Which of the following statements is NOT true concerning basic workplace etiquette?
    A. It's good practice to use eye contact and a firm handshake when meeting people for the first time.
    B. If you already know a person, it's not necessary to make proper introductions even if others

you are with don't know the person.

    C. Show up on time and stay on the job until it's time to leave.

    D. The person offering the invitation to a business lunch should foot the bill.

3. Which of the following statements is correct?

    A. It doesn't matter if your workspace is untidy.

    B. No one likes to wait while a co-worker attempts to unearth a missing item from under a mound of papers.

    C. You can talk about anything with your colleague when your boss is not in.

    D. It is a good idea to share personal or job-related problems with co-workers.

4. In order to maintain the perfect virtual meeting etiquette, which of the following do you need to follow?

    A. Expressing your opinions actively even if you are not asked to.

    B. Using inattentive body language if you're using your webcam.

    C. Turning on your microphone during the whole virtual meeting.

    D. Making proper eye contact in the camera.

5. What would be improper to do in the workplace?

    A. Take criticism personally.

    B. Borrow money from other co-workers.

    C. Take care of your private matters before you finish your work.

    D. All of the above.

Passage 2

Getting Along with Your Co-workers and the Boss

Getting along with your co-workers

Since you probably spend more time with your co-workers than with anyone else, it is essential to have, at least, a good relationship with them. Having good relationships in the workplace can make going to work a pleasure. Follow these tips to learn how to get along with your co-workers.

Be respectful to your co-workers

You don't have to be friends with all your colleagues, but you must demonstrate respect for one another by following the etiquette below.

• When engaging in conversations with co-workers inevitably in open office structures, keep your voice low so that you do not disturb others. Encourage each person to engage in discussion.

• Honor the schedules of your colleagues. Before starting a conversation, make sure that they have the time or want to talk at that moment.

• When you've been **requested** to attend a meeting, make sure you arrive on time or better, arrive early. Also, resisting your personal calls during a meeting is a smart idea. It shows you care for them, and that they can count on you.

• Do not indulge in rumors about other staff or the business in the office. Keep a safe distance between the professional and personal life of yourself and others too. When you're on personal time, hanging out with colleagues, talk of something light and positive rather than office gossip.

• Respect others' privacy. Don't read a co-worker's mail, or read memos or faxes on other people's desks or go through someone's desk unless it's absolutely necessary to do so, and don't make comments about overheard phone calls.

• Bring your healthy self to work. Leave "sick" germs at home to keep shared spaces and close working environments healthy for all.

• When making phone calls, either personal ones on your cell phone or job-related calls in your cubicle, don't distract anyone who is trying to work. Keep your voice down and have personal conversations in private.

• Clean up after yourself.

• Don't take anyone else's food from the refrigerator.

• Don't steal credit for someone else's work.

• If a co-worker tells you that a particular behavior annoys him or her, try your best to avoid it unless the request is unreasonable.

Speak less; listen more
Conflicts can sometimes **escalate** (加剧) from what started out as harmless word exchanges. Someone says a wrong word, or perhaps too much or too little, and then trouble begins to simmer.

Don't blab (闲扯) around your desk
If you're stuck next to someone who wants to chat with you on a nonstop basis, politely inform your colleague that the task at hand needs your attention but that you may have time to catch up at lunchtime or during a coffee break.

Work in a unique but complementary fashion
If you are working as a pair or in a team setting made up of employees with different styles of doing things, it may be a good idea to appoint tasks so that everyone can do his or her individual

part separately while getting feedback from the other members occasionally.

Avoid touchy subjects
No matter where you work, there are certain topics that should probably be avoided. These topics usually include politics, religion, and personal values, among others.

Allow for diversity
Some of your co-workers may differ from the majority due to race, ethnicity, gender, age, or other characteristics. Try to respect all differences within your work environment, and try to encourage others to do the same.

Strive for perfection
Try to go that extra step in dealing with co-workers in finding ways to ease strain and discouragement within the department. Try to keep a positive outlook whenever there's stress or difficulty. When employees support each other, they are less likely to engage in conflict with each other and can be easier to deal with.

It is important to get along with co-workers. Many top companies report that the ability to become a team player is one of the top three qualities sought in new hires. Make sure to keep your reputation unblemished by learning to appreciate other and **veering** (远离) away from potential conflicts.

Getting along with your boss
What bosses want is fairly simple. They want good employees, loyal, hardworking team players. Beyond this, what they expect in terms of respect is often more subtle and left to the employee to **discern** (察觉). The amount of respect bosses expect varies from office to office, but here are some general guidelines.

Show respect to your boss
Be slow to use first names. Until a boss tells you to call him "John" instead of "Mr. Leland," stick with the title, especially if you're young and newly hired. If the boss doesn't tell you what to call him, and you notice that everyone uses his first name, then after a few weeks or months on the job, you can switch to it, too. Beside, you should remember to let your boss go through doors and exit elevators ahead of you.

Let the boss take the lead in conversation
This doesn't mean you never start a conversation or that you don't say good morning, just that most of the time you take your cue from your boss. In general, bosses get to set the tone, time, place, and content of your conversations. It's **presumptuous** (冒昧的) for a mailroom clerk

(or almost any other employee) to take it upon himself to discuss golf, for example, with the chairman of the board while they're sharing an elevator.

Exercises

Choose the best answer to each question.

1. To get along well with your co-workers, you'd better _____.
    A. not interrupt others when engaging in conversations with co-workers
    B. keep to your own schedule strictly regardless of your colleagues' time
    C. keep an eye on your personal calls during a meeting
    D. indulge in rumors about other staff or the business in the office

2. Which of the following statements is NOT true when trying to get along with your co-workers?
    A. Don't distract anyone who is trying to work.
    B. Don't take anyone else's food from the refrigerator.
    C. Don't care when a co-worker tells you that your particular behavior annoys him or her.
    D. Don't steal credit for someone else's work.

3. When working with your co-workers, you need to _____.
    A. speak more and listen less
    B. chat with your co-workers on a nonstop basis
    C. concentrate on topics like politics, religion, and personal values
    D. work in a unique but complementary fashion

4. You should consider the suggestions below except _____.
    A. neglecting the differences within your work environment
    B. trying to keep a positive outlook whenever there's stress or a problem
    C. keeping your reputation clean by staying away from potential conflicts
    D. keeping a decent relationship with your co-workers

5. When getting along with your boss, you should _____.
    A. remember to exit elevators ahead of him or her
    B. remember to be careful when you use first names
    C. remember to take the lead in conversation
    D. remember to discuss golf if your boss likes it

SECTION 6 CULTURAL EXPLORATION

In this section, you will learn Chinese etiquette from the cultural perspective.

Task 1 Understanding Chinese etiquette in ancient poems or famous quotes

Read and study the following sayings of Confucius related to working culture in English from *Thus Spoke The Master* (Translated by Xu Yuanchong) and then find out their original Chinese versions. What messages are being conveyed in these sayings?

1. A good man never feels lonely; good neighbors will come up to him.

2. When you see a man better than you, you should try to equal him.

3. A cultured man may be slow in word but prompt in deed.

4. Impatience in minor matter may cause failure in main matter.

5. A craftsman who wishes to do his work well must first sharpen his tools.

6. Do not do to others what you would not have others do to you.

7. To admit what you know and what you do not know, that is knowledge.

8. When three men walk together, there must be one worthy to be my teacher.

Task 2 Learning Chinese traditions related to the etiquette of this unit

Read the short introduction to three characteristics of Chinese workplace culture and identify the major cultural points included in the passage. Then pick out some key words or cultural expressions that help you remember and understand the major points.

> China's workplace culture has been influenced greatly by the country's long-standing traditions and values. One of the most notable features of China's workplace culture is the strong executive ability of employees. Some people may think that Chinese employees are obedient to authority and willing to follow rules. However, the Chinese employees are encouraged to have their own ideas and opinions, and they are expected to contribute to

the success of their team and the company as a whole. In the process of understanding and executing tasks, they will look for the best methods and strategies and share information and experience with colleagues to complete tasks together. This collaborative approach to work is one of the reasons why many Chinese companies are so successful.

Another characteristic of China's workplace culture is the diligent work of employees. Chinese people have a long-standing belief that "heaven rewards hard work," which is deeply rooted in the Chinese culture. Chinese employees work long hours and are known for their strong work ethic. Many of them also continue to learn and improve their skills and knowledge after work or on weekends. They believe that only by constantly learning and improving can they stand out in fierce competition.

The third characteristic of China's workplace culture is that employees attach great importance to *guanxi* (interpersonal relationships). In China, building strong relationships with colleagues, superiors, and business partners is crucial to success in the workplace. Chinese employees are known for their politeness and respectfulness in their interactions with others. When expressing opinions in communication with colleagues, they will use gentle and polite language as much as possible and will not easily hurt others' face (reputation and social status). In dealing with superiors, they respect their decisions and opinions very much. They also understand the importance of maintaining good relationships outside the office. Chinese employees participate in various social activities in their spare time to consolidate and expand their network of contacts. These activities can enhance mutual understanding and friendship and can also exchange information and opinions.

1. Major cultural points in the story:
    (1) _____
    (2) _____
    (3) _____
2. Major words or cultural expressions in the story:
    (1) Para. 1 _____
    (2) Para. 2 _____
    (3) Para. 3 _____
3. What interesting stories about workplace culture would you like to share with your classmates?

Unit 8
Meeting Business Partners

You will learn in this unit

☐ behaving properly while meeting business partners

☐ greeting and addressing properly while meeting business partners

☐ dressing properly while meeting business partners

SECTION 1 INTRODUCTION

🎧 Listen to the following passage and fill in the blanks.

As countries of the world become increasingly 1._____ because of the global market and diverse 2._____, it is critically important for participating countries and their organizations to 3._____ one another's cultural differences in order to ensure growth and sustainability in international business. The business etiquette of different cultures vary due to people's 4._____ things such as time, space, and language habits, etc. When people of two cultures use time differently, 5._____ can generate misunderstanding, misinterpretation, and even ill will. Besides, people from the cultures that stress individualism generally 6._____ than do collective cultures. Business representatives from collective cultures place 7._____ on maintaining positive relations with their negotiation counterparts. To accomplish this, they rely on an indirect 8._____. Indirectness of this magnitude can be the source of consternation, confusion, and even misinterpretation to the 9._____, who is used to "getting to the point." In order to carry out effective cultural communication, proper 10._____ should be adopted to overcome the disadvantages of cultural differences and strengthen business cooperation.

SECTION 2 CHECK YOUR MANNERS

Read each of the following situations and choose the answer that best fits the circumstances.

1. You, a business consultant, are walking along with your client, the president of a company, and two of his employees, when you meet a business acquaintance of yours. Obviously it falls to you to introduce the four of them to each other. Whose name should you say first?
    A. The person standing on your immediate right.
    B. The person you've known the longest.
    C. The president of your client's company.
    D. Your business acquaintance.

2. Susan Ward has become a client of yours and you have a meeting scheduled so you can show her what your company can do for her. When you're speaking to her, you should refer to her as _____.
    A. Ms. Ward

B. Susan Ward

C. Susan

D. Susie, Baby

3. You have invited a client to a business lunch and upon arrival, a **maître d'**(领班) is waiting to escort you to your table. You should _____.

   A. let your guest follow behind the maître d' first

   B. walk ahead of your guest behind the maître d'

   C. ask your guest if he or she would like to go first

   D. forge ahead yourself and lead the entire group

4. You're attending a business buffet. Which of the following is proper etiquette while the honored guest speaks?

   A. Stop talking while carrying on eating.

   B. Keep talking with an important client.

   C. Walk around to find your client.

   D. Stop all activities such as taking or having food.

5. You encounter someone you've met before, but you can't remember his or her name. You should _____.

   A. turn around and leave and hope he or she didn't see you

   B. walk up to him or her and say, "Hi, what's your name?"

   C. walk up to him or her, use a generic greeting such as "Good morning" and just ignore the whole name issue

   D. walk up to him or her, use a generic greeting and admit that you don't remember his or her name

6. You have invited a business colleague to lunch. Who pays for the meal?

   A. You pay because you invited your colleague to lunch.

   B. Your business colleague pays because she accepted the invitation.

   C. Whichever one of you the waiter places the bill in front of pays.

   D. You go Dutch because that is the usual Western way.

7. If you must decline an invitation to a business event at the last minute, what should you do?

   A. Notify the host when you have time and express your regrets then.

   B. Inform the host prior to the event or first thing the next day with sincere regrets.

   C. Carry on with your more urgent work and apologize to the host when you meet him.

   D. Finish your work at hand first and apologize to the host when you are free.

8. At a business function that has a buffet, you choose to eat a mushroom appetizer served on a toothpick. What should you do with the toothpick when you're done?

   A. Put it back on the serving platter.

B. Put it in your napkin.

C. Surreptitiously drop it on the floor.

D. Keep it in the corner of your mouth.

9. When you receive someone else's business card you should _____.

   A. immediately stuff it into your pocket

   B. immediately pass them your business card

   C. look at the card and read it loudly

   D. look at the card and acknowledge it

10. When you are conversing with a business partner, you should stand _____.

    A. ten feet away from him

    B. six feet away from him

    C. three feet away from him

    D. one and a half feet away from him

SECTION 3   PRACTICE

In this part, proper etiquette will be learned through different tasks.

Task 1   Introducing people

Learning how to greet and address while meeting business partners is really important since it can help make a good start in business relationships. Decide what you should do in the following situation and complete the conversation.

Conversation

Harry Chan, an Asian employee in Ace Company, gets a task from his boss that he should escort one of the highest level executives of the company who comes over from USA. Chan is not very clear about greeting and introduction etiquette. He turns to Mary, one of his colleagues, for help.

(*In the office*)

Chan: Hi, Mary. Do you have a minute? I need your help.

Mary: Sure. What is it?

Chan: I'm going to accompany Mr. Johnson to a reception held by the clients this evening.

Mary: Well, aren't you flattered that your boss asked you to do that?

Chan: Yes, I am. Well, at the reception, I have to introduce Mr. Johnson to the clients. I'm not confident that I can do it correctly.

Mary: It's simple. You need to remember three rules. Rule No.1—always introduce people of 1._____ to people of 2._____.
Chan: I see. OK, rule No.2?
Mary: Rule No. 2 is to say the name of the most important person first.
Chan: Say the name of the most important person first. Well, 3._____ is the most important person.
Mary: No, as you introduce him to the clients, he is no longer the most important.
Chan: I see. Without clients we would have no business. So I should 4._____. What's the rule No. 3?
Mary: After telling the most important person's name, you should say "I would like to introduce so and so to you."
Chan: Let me try. Suppose the client is Mr. Smith, I should say "Mr. Smith, I would like to introduce you to Mr. Johnson." Is it right?
Mary: No. You should say: 5._____. How would you put it if you introduced me to Mr. Johnson?
Chan: I should say: 6._____.
Mary: That's correct. The difference is subtle but important. Can you tell the rules now?
Chan: OK. Rule No.1, always introduce people of lesser rank to people of greater rank; and Rule No. 2, say the name of the most important person first.
Mary: You've learnt Rule No.3, too. OK, you're all set. Good luck tonight and enjoy!

Task 2 Thinking differently of body language

Good body language is part of good conversation. Body language tells a lot about a person's character, such as whether he shows respect for others to whom he is talking, and whether he pays proper attention to someone else's ideas. In business interactions, proper body language may add a lot to the possibility of your success. Read the following statements and say how Western people think about certain kinds of behavior.

Gestures	The westerners think
1. While shaking hands, one uses the other hand to support the handshaking wrist.	1. <u>It's a sign of humbleness and respect</u>.
2. While being introduced to someone, stand up and squarely face the person to whom you are being introduced before shaking hands.	2. _____
3. While speaking to someone, keep a physical distance of 2 feet.	3. _____

4. While sitting in a meeting, slump down on your backbone and your legs straight out in front of you.

4. _____

5. While listening, watch the face of the person speaking.

5. _____

6. While sitting, shift your position or cross and uncross your knees.

6. _____

7. While standing, stick your belly out, put your hands in your pockets, or fold your arms.

7. _____

8. While speaking, one scratches his nose.

8. _____

9. While speaking, one crosses his hands and makes sounds.

9. _____

10. Receiving a cup of tea or a business card with only one hand.

10. _____

11. After giving a speech, clap together with the audience.

11. _____

Task 3 Performing in business situations

Work in pairs and role-play the following situations. Make certain you know how to behave properly in these situations.

Situation 1

Harry Chan is attending a networking event. He wants to meet more business people who might be potential business partners in the near future. He decides to introduce himself to some "approachable" people first. Chan gets to know more than 10 people after 1 hour. There is also an embarrassing moment for him when he speaks to a lady he has just met. One of the lady's friends approaches them but that lady does not introduce them to each other. What do you think he should do?

Situation 2

Harry Chan bought a new suit last week because he found all the highest level executives dress themselves formally even on hot days. Amy says he looks nice in the new suit and it is always good to imitate the way the highest level executives dress. Americans have a saying about business attire: "Dress for the job you want, not the job you have." "Would you mind if I pointed out a few things you could do to improve your look even more?" Amy comments that Chan did a good job selecting the suit but the length of his pants is not enough. She also gives good advice about dressier shoes to match the suit, a V-neck style undershirt on hot days, no bare feet and no white socks.

Task 4 Talking about culture differences

Work in groups to find out different concepts of time between Chinese and Western people.

Time Concept in Business Negotiations

Time in China is a very important concept, and all Chinese know the Confucian proverb: "Think three times before you act." Not being hasty is a sign of wisdom and sincerity. As China has a long history, Chinese people find it normal to take a long-range view of events and are less likely to be rushed when they face decisions. Negotiators usually stress the process rather than how long it takes to get there. So they may make concession until the last minute of negotiations.

While a basic assumption of Western negotiation is that the faster that money or goods change hands, the greater the increase in value and the larger the profits. The Western negotiators want to make a deal quickly, then another. Short-term transactions are valued. They are known for their speed and strive for getting through the content of the negotiations as efficiently as possible. They always seem to be in a hurry and under pressure for results. Most Westerners have very low tolerance for extensions and postponements if there is a schedule.

SECTION 4 CASE STUDY

Read the following cases and do each case study in small groups. The questions in "Critical thinking" after each case are aimed to help with finding the story background, the problem itself, the etiquette involved, and the cultural differences behind the etiquette. Remember to provide possible solutions to the problem in each case.

Case 1

The Aftermath of a Luxury Dinner Party

A state-owned enterprise was going to negotiate a business deal with a big American company. The enterprise did a lot of research about the company and had prepared everything well before they invited the delegates. The boss of the company was given a tour of the manufacturing workshop, technology center and other important places. The enterprise's equipment, technology and workers' operating skills were highly praised by him. People from the enterprise were delighted with the feedback and decided to host a dinner party in honor of the visitor. The dinner took place in a very luxurious restaurant and was attended by more than twenty middle managements from the enterprise as well as some city leaders. The American boss had thought that there would be other guests and activities. He couldn't understand the situation when he heard that he was the only guest and expressed immediately that he had to re-consider his relationship with the enterprise. After the American boss left, he sent a fax to the enterprise declining any offer. The refusal baffled the enterprise since they thought that they had met all the requirements of the American company, and they had given a good reception and shown good hospitality to the American boss.

Critical thinking

1. Retell the case in 3–4 sentences using the expressions in the box.

a state-owned enterprise	negotiate with	highly praised
a very luxurious restaurant	declining any offer	feel baffled

2. Suppose you were the boss, write a reply to the enterprise leaders explaining why they were refused.

3. Do people from collectivism and people from individualism understand the sincerity in doing business in the same way? Please give your opinions.

Case 2

Blair and Andy meet in the office the morning after a business dinner.

Blair: Hi, Andy. How are you?

Andy: I'm fine, thank you, and you?

Blair: I'm very tired. My boss Mr. Brown and I went to a business dinner with clients yesterday evening, and we got back very late.

Andy: Did everything go all right?

Blair: Well, I think one client did not conduct himself well.

Andy: What did he do?

Blair: As soon as we took our seats, he took off his coat and put it on the back of the chair. It was a bit hot in the restaurant, but Mr. Brown hadn't taken off his coat, so I hadn't either.

Andy: That's a good thing because unless your host, in this case, Mr. Brown, removes his jacket, you should not remove yours.

Blair: The client apparently hadn't thought of that. But Andy, I remember you once told me that we should try to let the clients feel at ease.

Andy: Yes, I did. That's all part of good manners. Why do you ask?

Blair: Because after a while, the client found that he was the only person who wasn't wearing a coat, so he felt very awkward. If I were the host, I surely would take off the coat after him.

Andy: I agree with you. Sometimes you need to do things that you wouldn't normally do to put other people at ease.

Blair: If I were Mr. Brown, when seeing the client taking off his coat, I would say "it is a bit too hot for me indeed to put on the coat."

Andy: Absolutely. That would have made your client feel comfortable and given everyone permission to do the same. Tell me what else happened at dinner. It sounds like quite an interesting night.

Blair: Oh, when the soup was served, that client tossed his tie over his shoulder. I guess he didn't want to get his tie dirty.

Andy: That is definitely not acceptable under any circumstances. Most men have forgotten that ties were originally created to protect the shirt. Not only is it out of place to toss your tie over your shoulder at the table, it runs counter to its purpose.

Blair: I see. A tie is used to protect the shirt. Then, can we tuck a napkin under the chin?

Andy: Good heavens, no. Your napkin should be laid on your lap—never tucked in anywhere.

Blair: Really? I once saw a lot of people with their napkin tucked in under the chin. I nearly did the same last night!

Andy: Thank goodness you did not.

Critical thinking

1. Retell the case in 3–4 sentences using the expressions in the box.

dinner party	client	conduct himself well	took off
feel at ease	awkward	put other people at ease	
tossed his tie over his shoulder		tuck a napkin under the chin	

2. Why did Blair think the client did not conduct himself well during the business dinner?

3. Do you think differently from Blair about the clients' manners during the business dinner? Why?

SECTION 5 READING FOR ETIQUETTE TIPS

Read the following passages and finish the exercises after each of the texts.

Passage 1

Business Etiquette for Corporate Events

Appropriate business etiquette is expected of all professionals, especially at corporate events. However, few individuals are trained in the art of good manners. That means most people learn meeting etiquette and how to conduct themselves at business events "on the job."

Of course, not everyone is completely at ease with knowing whether they are conveying proper business etiquette to corporate hosts, colleagues and other guests.

Keep in mind, the purpose of etiquette is to create an environment that allows everyone to feel comfortable. The following Q&A provides some business etiquette tips for different meeting environments.

When should you respond to an RSVP?
Event invitations will provide most of the important information of the event, including details about the host, type of event, purpose (even as much as a brief agenda), location, time, specific instructions, and—of course—the RSVP. Events today rely on a variety of RSVP options, including email, phone, cards, letters and others. It is important for guests to respond quickly when they receive an invitation, and it's best to respond within a week. If you must decline at the last minute, please notify the host prior to the event or first thing the next day with sincere apologies.

What should you wear to an event?
Hosts and guests err on the side of conservative dress: dress well and in good taste (everything should always be pressed). That said, most event invitations will provide direction:
- Business **attire** (服装) (suits and dresses)
- Black tie/black tie optional (more formal evening wear)
- Business casual (trousers/khakis with long sleeve shirts)
- Jackets and ties required (as instructed)

Some events and venues may advise other casual wear, such as golf, tennis, horse racing, resorts, etc. Organizers will be specific about attire requirements.

When should you arrive for an event?
The event host would have spent a significant time and resources to plan and execute an event, so most people know the answer to this question: be on time! If you are a representative of the host, the answer is that you should arrive up to 30 minutes early (you will be given a time and you should show up when requested).

If you are a guest, understand that the organizer has been selective with the invitation list. Many invitations will include a brief agenda that highlights when guests may arrive for the event, typically providing a window of 15 to 30 minutes for registration and welcome reception lines. Also, it's important to stay as long as possible or to the conclusion of an event.

When should you extend a handshake at an event?
Always upon arrival and departure. This is an easy rule that few people violate. Greet everyone with a firm, sincere handshake, a friendly smile and direct eye contact. However, when approaching a group of individuals, it's important to note that guests should always shake the hand of the host first.

Of course, there are **scenarios** (情景) when handshake greetings aren't possible, such as when both hands are full. In those situations, either party may nod and use some sort of other body gesture to convey the greeting.

How should you introduce people in a group at an event?
Most people will find themselves at some point introducing various individuals at an event, especially when they are the ones who will be expected to know all parties. But what's the order of introductions? Simply remember two rules:
- Introduce lower ranking individuals to higher ranking individuals.
- Remember to include titles (e.g., Dr., Judge, etc.) and name prefix (e.g., Mr., Mrs. or Ms.).

What should you talk about at the event?
It's important to have strong listening (don't interrupt) and conversation skills in group situations. This means maintaining open body language (stand up or sit up straight, don't cross your arms, and maintain good eye contact) and showing interest in what others have to say.

Contribute to conversations by being able to speak on a variety of subjects, try to find topics of mutual interest and avoid correcting what others have to say. Make sure to involve everyone in the group in the discussion (and not just one or two). Encourage people to talk about themselves, and be graceful when providing and/or accepting compliments.

It's unfortunate to add the following, but necessary for some: avoid the use of **foul** (污秽的) language and slang in conversations.

What shouldn't you talk about at the event?

Just as it's important to understand what to talk about, there are several topics that should generally be avoided:

- Personal finances
- Personal health (yours and others)
- Divisive topics
- Gossip

How should you show your respect?

It may sound old fashioned, but it's very important to let people know that you hold them in high esteem. And the act will usually not go unnoticed by the recipient. Several examples (but certainly not an all inclusive list) of when politeness is important at an event:

- Follow the lead of others (e.g., host) to know when/where to sit.
- Hold doors for others.
- Don't assume empty seats are available.
- Allow others to take the better seat.
- Wait to speak until others acknowledge you.
- Wait for the host before taking a first drink.
- Wait to eat until after everyone is served and the host has begun.

Exercises

Choose the best answer to each question.

1. When meeting business partners, the purpose of etiquette is not to _____.
    A. make the situation formal and the interaction applaudable
    B. create an environment that allows everyone to feel comfortable
    C. show off a noble life style even in business
    D. leave a good impression on each other

2. Most event invitations will not provide information about _____.
    A. the host
    B. pets
    C. attire
    D. type of event

3. According to the passage, when approaching a group of individuals in a business event, it's important to note that _____.
    A. guests should always shake the hand of the host first

B. the host should always extend his hand first

C. the host should always shake the hand of the most important person

D. guests should always wait to be introduced

4. When introducing people in a group at an event, _____.

   A. you give your name card to the one you introduce first

   B. you ask them to introduce themselves to each other

   C. you introduce higher ranking individuals to lower ranking individuals

   D. you introduce lower ranking individuals to higher ranking individuals

5. What shouldn't you talk about at the event?

   A. Personal finances.

   B. Personal health (yours and others).

   C. Gossip.

   D. All the above.

Passage 2

Business Dinner Parties

Dining with clients is part of business activities. The following are some tips for you while attending business dinners.

Does a buffet mean I can do what I want?

Certainly not. A buffet is one of the main kinds of business dinners, the other being formal dinner party. You have to be careful about your manners on both occasions.

There are generally honored guests and the host at a buffet. The host makes an **extemporaneous** (即席的) speech first. While the honored guest speaks, everyone should stop all activities such as taking or having food. Generally, a buffet is not like a Chinese dinner or a Western formal dinner party which involves the arrangement of the seats, so people could walk around. When talking with others, try not to chew food in your mouth; when taking food, do not pile it up on your plate. Although you are free to take whatever food you like, it doesn't mean you could waste food.

How should I behave at a formal dinner party, esp. with my boss or some important clients?

Formal business dinners or lunches **entail** (需要) double effort—being in business while watching your table manners. Here are some tips on how to behave properly if you are dining out with your boss.

• Act professionally. You, operating outside office hours and outside the **office premises** (办公场所), don't give you license to let your hair down. You are still technically at work and you do not want to leave a negative impression on your boss (or horror of horrors, an important client). You don't want to **blurt** (未加思索地冲口说出) out all your secrets, especially your secret hatred for your boss, do you? Drink in moderation. Otherwise, you'll find yourself being fired the next day for calling your boss names while drunk the night before.

• Be charming, but let your boss be on center stage. Impress your boss by being witty and **congenial** (意气相投的). But if you have other people with you, curb your enthusiasm a bit and let your boss be under the spotlight.

• If you are going to take your spouse or partner, prepare them beforehand. Make sure that they know what to discuss and what not to discuss during dinner. Of course, if your spouse is as tactful as you are, they will refrain from saying anything that will put your job on the line.

• Dress **conservatively** (保守地). Sure, you can look great but try not to look like you're going to **seduce** (诱惑) everyone in attendance.

• As for the **tab** (标签), whoever usually arranged the meal should pay, normally the boss. However, you should pay if you are dining with a client. If it's with colleagues, then going Dutch is okay. Whatever the arrangement is, try not to **squabble** (争吵) about it. Be gracious if you are being treated.

• Mind your table manners. Dining, is still dining, whether it is for business or not. Good table manners still apply.

Where should I sit?

The seats at the business dinner party table would generally tell the importance of the people. In most Western countries, the seat of the right is taken for respect. A female guest of honor usually sits to the right hand side of the host, while a male guest of honor usually sits to the right hand side of the hostess. The following pictures may guide you to find your seat according to your position. If someone could meet you at the gate and guide you to the right seat, you could save the efforts.

Unit 8 Meeting Business Partners

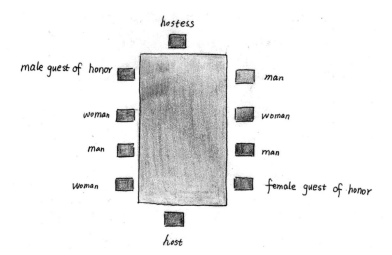

Exercises

Choose the best answer to each question.

1. What is a buffet like when it is a business dinner?
   A. It is semi-formal, with food and drinks served for free.
   B. Guests come to have a good meal and enjoy their time with friends.
   C. Guests walk around and chat while eating and drinking.
   D. Guests appear in their most fashionable suits or dresses.

2. What is appropriate for you to do at a buffet?
   A. As the host, you give a brimful speech that you have prepared well to welcome the guests.
   B. As the honored guest, you give a speech too, long and full of enthusiasm to show your appreciation.
   C. As a guest, you should keep quiet and listen carefully to the one who is making a speech.
   D. As a guest, you are free to take whatever food you like and pile it up on your plate.

3. How should you behave properly at a formal dinner party with some important clients?
   A. You are prepared to have a drink with your clients.
   B. You act respectfully and professionally like you are still at work.
   C. You bring your partner to the party and tell them to cotton up to the clients.
   D. You pay for the meal even if the dinner is arranged by the clients.

4. How should you behave at a formal dinner party at which your boss is present?
   A. You try to impress your boss by being the focus of attention.
   B. You dress yourself in smart and conservative business attire for the occasion.
   C. You are ready to take over some drinks intended for your boss in case he gets drunk.
   D. You never let your boss pay for the meal even if he insists.

143

5. At a formal Western style dinner party, which of the following is the best seating arrangement?
   A. The host will take the seat next to the hostess.
   B. The hostess will seat herself next to female guests.
   C. The honored male guest will be seated to the left of the host to show respect.
   D. The honored female guest will be seated to the right of the host to show respect.

Passage 3

Understanding Cultural Differences in Business Etiquette

Basic knowledge and practice of etiquette is a valuable advantage to have, because in a lot of situations, a second chance may not be possible or practical. There are many written and unwritten rules and guidelines for etiquette, and it certainly **behooves** (对…有必要) a business person to learn them. The **caveat** (警告) is that there is no possible way to know all of them! These guidelines have some difficult-to-navigate **nuances** (细微差别), depending on the company, the local culture, and the requirements of the situation. Possibilities to commit a **faux pas** (失礼, 失态) are limitless, and chances are, sooner or later, you'll make a mistake. But one can minimize them, recover quickly, and avoid causing a bad impression by being generally considerate and attentive to the concerns of others, and by adhering to the basic rules of etiquette. When in doubt one ought to stick to the basics. This last **assertion** (主张, 声明) entails a **legitimate** (合法的) question: what does one understand by basics both for business etiquette and politeness?

First of all, it is wise to research the national and local business culture beforehand because having insight into the cultural dynamics of a country or region can be very helpful to understand why people act the way they do, and the appropriate way you should act while in that country. There are three areas that should be considered regardless of cultural differences: appearance, which highlights business etiquette do's and don'ts involving dress, body language, and gestures; behavior, which highlights business etiquette do's and don'ts involving dining, gift-giving, meetings, customs, **protocol** (协议), negotiation, and general behavioral guidelines; and communication, which highlights business etiquette do's and don'ts involving greetings, introductions, and conversational guidelines.

These three areas mentioned above and their cultural characteristics stem from four primary dimensions to **differentiate** (区别) cultures, identified by Geert Hofstede and his model analysis:
- The Power Distance Index (PDI) focuses on the degree of equality, or inequality, between people in the country's society.
- The Individualism (IDV) focuses on the degree the society reinforces individual or collective, achievement and interpersonal relationships.

- The **Masculinity** (阳刚之气) (MAS) focuses on the degree the society reinforces, or does not reinforce, the traditional masculine work role model of male achievement, control, and power.
- The Uncertainty Avoidance Index (UAI) focuses on the level of tolerance for uncertainty and **ambiguity** (不明确) within the society—i.e. unstructured situations.

To these four dimensions, Geert Hofstede added the following fifth dimension after conducting an additional international study using a survey instrument developed with Chinese employees and managers. That survey resulted in an addition to the Confucian dynamism. Subsequently, Hofstede described that dimension as a culture's long-term orientation. Long-Term Orientation (LTO) focuses on the degree the society embraces, or does not embrace long-term devotion to traditional, forward thinking values.

Geert Hofstede's dimensions analysis can assist the business person or traveler in better understanding the intercultural differences within regions and between countries and in choosing the most appropriate code for business communication. The rules that govern this code are influenced and assisted, in my opinion, by business etiquette and politeness. Irrespective of the country analyzed by using the above-mentioned dimensions, the conclusion one can draw is that the differences are significantly relevant and the only possible solution is to turn to some basic assumptions, already mentioned, not far from what the etiquette exhibits. For example, the most important thing to remember is to be courteous and thoughtful to the people around, regardless of the situation.

It is also advisable to consider other people's feelings and stick to one's **convictions** (确信) as diplomatically as possible. Moreover, it is advisable to address conflict as situation-related, rather than person-related. Apologize whenever the case. There will be no doubt that what one says will be much more effective because it carries the weight of **credibility** (可信性) and respectability.

The general topics addressed by business etiquette deal with: people, first and foremost; peers and **subordinates** (下级); superiors; international business; the workplace; meetings; the phone; email; interruptions; guests, consultants and new employees; appreciation/credit; dress/appearance; social settings; introductions; table manners. With this general picture at hand, cultural differences can be carefully addressed and possible conflicts overcome.

Exercises

Choose the best answer to each question.

1. According to the passage, which of the following cannot help people minimize improper behaviors in business situations?
    A. Being generally considerate and attentive to the concerns of others.
    B. Adhering to the basic rules of etiquette.
    C. Considering other people's feelings.
    D. Sticking to one's own preference on business issues.

2. According to the passage, which of the following should be considered in order to understand why people act the way they do?
    A. Their education background.
    B. Their family background.
    C. The city which they come from.
    D. The specifics of national business culture.

3. According to the passage, the areas of interest which account for the impact of business etiquette include all the following except for _____.
    A. behavior
    B. appearance
    C. family
    D. communication

4. Which of the following dimensions of Geert Hofstede's model involved Chinese employees and managers?
    A. The Power Distance Index.
    B. Long-Term Orientation.
    C. The Masculinity.
    D. The Uncertainty Avoidance Index.

5. The first and foremost topic addressed by business etiquette deals with _____.
    A. the workplace
    B. peers and subordinates
    C. people
    D. dress/appearance

Unit 8　Meeting Business Partners

SECTION 6　CULTURAL EXPLORATION

In this section, you will learn Chinese etiquette from the cultural perspective.

Task 1　Understanding Chinese etiquette in ancient poems or famous quotes

Read and study the following ancient Chinese poem related to working banquet in English and then find out its original Chinese version. What message is being conveyed in this poem?

The Heavy Dew(Excerpt)
From Book of Songs
By anonymity
Translated by Xu Yuanchong

Bright is the heavy dew,
On date and willow trees.
Our noble guests are true,
And good at perfect ease.

The plane and jujube trees,
Have their fruits hanging down.
Our noble guests will please,
In manner and renown.

_____
作者_____
译者_____

_____
_____
_____
_____
_____
_____

Task 2 Learning Chinese traditions related to the etiquette of this unit

Read the following introduction to Shanxi merchants in Chinese history and identify the major cultural points included in the passage. Then pick out some key words or cultural expressions that help you remember and understand the major points.

> The term "Shanxi merchants" refers to Shanxi merchants in the Ming and Qing dynasties, together with Chaozhou merchants and Huizhou merchants. In Chinese history these are called the "three major merchants" in Chinese history.
>
> In the early Ming Dynasty, nine important border garrisons were set up and the law of salt was issued. Shanxi merchants were allowed to pay taxes in grain to transport salt, and their commercial activities gradually rose. Later, with the expansion of their businesses, their footprints were all over the country. In the Qing Dynasty, Shanxi merchants opened up the "Ten Thousand Miles Tea Road" and the trade became international. In the early years of Daoguang Period in the Qing Dynasty, Shanxi merchants founded the first draft bank in Chinese history in Pingyao, which combined commercial and financial capital. Shanxi banks were located in major domestic commercial towns, and their business activities also spread overseas. Shanxi merchants had good credit, conducting financial exchanges all over the world and becoming the leading force in finance for nearly a hundred years.
>
> Shanxi merchants have been in the business world for around five hundred years, leaving a rich cultural heritage and an inexhaustible spiritual wealth.

1. Major cultural points in the story:

    (1) _____

    (2) _____

2. Major words or cultural expressions in the story:

    (1) Para. 1 _____

    (2) Para. 2 _____

    (3) Para. 3 _____

3. What interesting stories about Shanxi merchants or other Chinese businessman stories would you like to share with your classmates?

Unit 9
Attending a Wedding Ceremony

You will learn in this unit
- [ ] wedding guest attire
- [ ] bride and groom attire
- [ ] wedding toast etiquette
- [ ] wedding guest manners

SECTION 1 INTRODUCTION

🎧 **Listen to the following passage and fill in the blanks.**

Wedding traditions from all over the world prove that humans are social beings supporting one another towards the success of society, especially in the formation of 1._____ —the family, which starts with the union of husband and wife. Despite this, wedding traditions 2._____ from country to country. When attending a wedding in Western countries, it is important to be aware of and respect the cultural differences when you enter into a 3._____. One of the biggest challenges is the different communication styles, ranging from 4._____, such as different ways to use words and phrases, to various forms of 5._____ communication, which include not only facial expressions, but also 6._____, sense of time, and personal distance.

Proposing a toast, for example, is 7._____ of all wedding receptions worldwide. Although the speech displays joy over the marriage, it also shows some differences between 8._____. The wedding speech in some cultures tells stories about the bride and groom 9._____; whereas, in other cultures, the wedding speech, made by the parents of the bride and groom, usually 10._____ about family life, and how the couple should treat each other during the marriage.

SECTION 2 CHECK YOUR MANNERS

Read the following statements, then mark T for the true statements and F for the false statements. Provide corrections for the false ones.

__ 1. It is not rude to be unable to attend a wedding. Do send a gift though, even if you can't make it.

__ 2. Respect the sanctity of the marriage ritual, taking photographs during the ceremony is acceptable.

__ 3. A gift is required every time you are invited to a wedding ceremony. But there is no dollar amount you must hit with a wedding gift.

__ 4. While a wedding is a time to enjoy oneself, no one appreciates a drunk guest embarrassing themselves.

__ 5. After you are invited to a wedding, send the wedding gift to the couple ahead of time, so they don't have to lug it home from the reception. However, if you don't attend, the gift is not required.

___ 6. Your most important obligation as a guest is to respond to the invitation immediately, if you are unable to attend.

___ 7. Arrive at the ceremony on time, preferably the exact time it's scheduled to start.

___ 8. Leave at least before the wedding cake is cut. Do not leave without saying goodbye and thanking at least a member of the couple's immediate family, if you can't reach the couple themselves.

___ 9. You are related to the bride or groom and you talk about the wedding, as well as the bride and groom's exes.

___ 10. Do not wear black to a wedding because it is too gloomy, while white is appropriate.

SECTION 3 PRACTICE

In this section, proper etiquette will be learned through different tasks.

Task 1 Dressing for a wedding ceremony

Have you ever felt confused as to what to wear to attend a certain type of wedding? Work in pairs to match the appropriate attire with different types of event in the table below.

Type of event	No.	Him	Her
1. The most formal	A	**tuxedo** (无尾晚礼服), black bow tie, **cummerbund** (宽腰带), patent leather shoes	neutral-color cocktail dress or long evening gown in a dark color
2. Second most formal	B	suit and tie	cocktail dress, dressy skirt and top
3. Formal	C	summer suit with a linen shirt (no ties required), linen pants, sandals	tea- or knee-length formal summer sundress, flat sandals
4. Beach Formal	D	tuxedo, long jacket with tails, white pique vest, bow tie, formal black shoes, white gloves	formal full-length neutral-color ball gown, dressy jewelry and hair
5. Semiformal	E	dress pants, button-down shirt, **polo** (马球装)	summer sundress, skirt or pants with a nice blouse
6. Casual	F	tuxedo, formal dark suit and tie	long dress, dressy suit, formal cocktail-length dress in neutral colors

Task 2 Learning wedding expressions
Complete the short paragraph and test what you know about the wedding etiquette.

> honeymoon   wife   husband   bride
> groom   cake   invitation   reception

Before you go to a wedding, you must receive an 1._____. The people getting married are called the 2._____ and 3._____. After the wedding, there is a special party called a 4._____. There is usually lots of food and a special 5._____. After the wedding the 6._____ and his new 7._____ usually go on a special holiday called a 8._____.

Task 3 Being a well-mannered wedding guest
Look at the descriptions and then decide which behaviors are acceptable and which are unacceptable for a wedding guest. Then explain why you think so.

Situation 1: Reply to the host or hostess whether you plan to attend as soon as you receive an invitation.

My ideas: _____

Unit 9 Attending a Wedding Ceremony

Situation 2: Bring the gift with you when you attend a wedding.

My ideas: _____

Situation 3: When attending a wedding ceremony, you bring your boyfriend even if he is not invited.

My ideas: _____

Situation 4: You dress yourself in a white and shining dress to a wedding ceremony.

My ideas: _____

Situation 5: You take pictures all the time at a wedding ceremony so that you can share the sweet moment of the bride and bridegroom with friends in the future.

My ideas: _____

Task 4 Talking about the wedding ceremony

Complete the conversations with the words or expressions necessary for each occasion, then role-play them with a partner.

| on the right side | fell in love | good news | a civil ceremony |
| on the left side | the big day | the best man | the bridegroom |

Conversation 1

James: Hi, Lily, I have some 1._____ for you.

Lily: What's that?

James: Jessica is getting married.

Lily: That's great! Who's 2._____?

James: Bob, that lucky guy.

Lily: When did he propose?

James: Last week. It is said that he 3._____ with Jessica at Mrs. Smith's party last Monday as soon as he saw her.

Lily: My God! How romantic! When's 4._____?

James: July 4th.

Lily: Will it be a church wedding or 5._____?

James: Jessica plans to hold it in church.

Lily: Who is 6._____?

James: Guess!

Lily: Nobody is better than you!

James: You know, Bob is my best friend and he asked me to be his best man.
Lily: Did you promise him?
James: Yes, I did.

Conversation 2

Jessica: Excuse me, in my wedding ceremony, where do my parents sit in the church?

Church Staff: Let me see. The bride's parents' seating arrangement is 7._____ of the aisle and the groom's parents are 8._____.

Jessica: Fine. Then do friends of the bride always sit on one side of the church and friends of the groom on the other?

Church Staff: Yes, they usually do.

SECTION 4   CASE STUDY

Read the following cases and do each case study in small groups. The questions in "Critical thinking" after each case are aimed to help with finding the story background, the problem itself, the etiquette involved, and the cultural differences behind the etiquette. Remember to provide possible solutions to the problem in each case.

Case 1

Unsuccessful Wedding Toast

Story 1

My husband's brother is well known for his selfishness. He was the best man at our wedding and gave the worst toast you could ever imagine. The speech was typed, single-spaced, on 5 pages, front and back. It lasted about 20 minutes and I (the bride) don't recall being mentioned once. The theme of the speech was "I'm losing my brother" and contained gems like "I can't believe he is getting married," "It's going to be so weird" and "we won't be able to hang out anymore." I was not welcomed to the family, not congratulated, not spoken to or looked at. And we get along just fine—it wasn't intended to be disrespectful. Apparently, he's just a bad toaster.

He went on and on about how his parents sacrificed and drove crappy cars when they were little so they could provide for their kids and how much HE appreciated this. And how he (and the groom) were involved in sports and their parents would buy them all the gear and take them to their games. And that his parents had paid for the groom's dinner the night before and how they were also paying for the groom's dinner at HIS wedding, four months later, all while they were trying to retire. All of this is lovely ... but what does it have to do with our wedding?

And there was just no end in sight. It had been 20 minutes; he was only on page 2 and was clearly adlibbing at this point. I'm looking around the room and seeing people staring in disbelief. People are rolling their eyes and waiting for this miserable toast to end. So, I nudged my husband and told him to interrupt. He ran up and hugged him and said "thank you" mid-sentence and took the microphone away, receiving a very large, thankful round of applause from the guests. I believe my brother-in-law's heart was in the right place, but his mind was not present. It really upset me, because after THAT toast, no one else wanted to follow, so the toasts ended and we didn't get any fun stories or congratulations. Friends and family from both sides later told us they wanted to say something but didn't dare after that lengthy toast.

Story 2

At our rehearsal dinner, after the lovely, well-wishing and touching speeches given by my husband's family and friends, my family and friends started to stand up and put in their words. While their speeches were intended to be well wishing and funny, they made me want to crawl under the table.

My father said that he was proud of my accomplishments and wished me well. Then he said that there wasn't much more he could say about me, because I spent my entire childhood in my room, and the groom probably knew me better than he did.

One of my bridesmaids, one of my best friends from college, stood up and stated that for as long as she has known me, I have been a wonderful friend, and I would do anything for anybody. Then she said that I had a "long, spotty dating history," that I have been "hurt many times over," and that she was so glad that I was marrying my husband because he "fulfilled a large void" in my life that needed filling.

Then another one of my bridesmaids, a great friend from high school, stood up. She said that she has seen me grow up into a mature, successful person (nice) ... after my string of "bad prior relationships" (groan). My father added from his seat at the table, loud enough for everyone to hear that I just decided on the guy who refurbished my kitchen for me.

Then my two sisters stood up. My younger sister gave a truly lovely speech about the bond and lifetime friendship between sisters. Everything she said was very nice. When she finished, my older sister chimed up, "Brian, we're just glad it's you."

We tried to make our own speech but we never actually made our way through it. My husband tried to thank everyone and broke down with emotion. Then I teared up, and we held each other. I think that said it all.

Critical thinking

1. Retell the case in 3–4 sentences using the expressions in the box.

Story 1	best man 20 minutes bride not mentioned theme of the speech not have to do with wedding waiting for miserable toast to end not get congratulations
Story 2	touching speeches crawl under the table not much more about me long spotty dating history sting of "bad prior relationships" bond and lifetime friendship chime up

2. Do the people in the two stories make proper wedding toasts? Why? What would you say if you were one of them to make a toast at the wedding?

3. What are the cultural differences behind the wedding toasts in Chinese and Western weddings?

Case 2

Unpleasant Guests

Story 1

I recently attended a wedding with my boyfriend. It was a nice wedding and very tastefully done, but I was blown away by the guests' behavior at the reception. First of all, when we got to the reception there were obviously more people there than were at the wedding—meaning they either gate-crashed the reception or were invited but declined to go to the wedding OR the bride only invited them to the reception; regardless something went wrong somewhere. Some of these people even came in jeans, which is just tacky. So, being that there were more people than at the wedding, there were not enough seats for everyone to sit down and eat after going through the buffet line. The wedding cake and the groom's cake were at the very front of the reception hall and the guests actually used the tables that these cakes were sitting on to eat. Not sure if this is a faux pas, but I have never seen this done before. I thought it was a little rude.

The worst thing that I saw, which my boyfriend and I were both pretty appalled at, was this: On the table by the groom's cake was a little tower of chocolate covered strawberries decorated to match the cake. Guests, and I am not talking children or teenagers, but grown men and women, were taking them and eating them. This was before any cake had been cut, not to mention there was a table of sweets provided after the buffet. A woman took one and put it on her plate and right after she did it, her little girl (maybe 4 or 5) followed suit. When the mother and father saw this, they said "NO! NO! NO!! You can't have that!" and proceeded to put it back on the table with the other strawberries.

Story 2

I was married in Anchorage, Alaska in 1973. While the city is not stuck in the gold rush days, some of the guests apparently were. We had a civil ceremony at the courthouse with only us and our two witnesses (a best man and a matron of honor). To share our happiness, my husband and I decided to throw a wedding "reception" for our friends three weeks after the actual wedding. Since we had spent most of our "dating" at the small ski lodge where my hubby worked, we decided to have our party there. It was in early May so the lodge was closed and the snow was almost gone. Most of the guests were my hubby's friends who worked with him at the lodge. My mom and I planned a modest affair with some party trays and snacks, a large 4-tiered wedding cake, champaigne and lots of spiked punch. I wasn't planning a formal affair but I expected my guests to come to a wedding reception in nice party clothes. About a third of the guests showed up in flannel shirts and blue jeans! That was tacky enough but one guest out-did the others in tackiness. He and his wife showed up in their casual clothes, i.e., flannel shirts and blue jeans, and upon entering the lodge he loudly asked, "Anyone want to take a ride in my new Budweiser canoe? I have it with me!" For those who don't remember, Budweiser had just released some TV commercials featuring a canoe covered with Budweiser labels. He apparently was very proud of his reproduction. Fortunately, none of the guests took him up on the ride.

Critical thinking

1. Retell the case in 3–4 sentences using the expressions in the box.

Story 1	attend a wedding blown away obviously more people tacky not enough seats rude worst thing put back on the table
Story 2	civil ceremony wedding reception ski lodge modest affair nice party clothes tacky

2. What behaviors in the two stories made the hosts and hostesses think the guests are unpleasant? What is the proper etiquette for guests when attending a Chinese wedding party?

3. What are the cultural differences behind guest etiquette in Chinese and Western wedding parties?

SECTION 5 READING FOR ETIQUETTE TIPS

Read the following passages and finish the exercises after each of the texts.

Passage 1

Western Style Wedding Etiquette for Guests

When your friends or family get married, there are all kinds of wedding etiquette and rules that govern their behavior. But did you know there are rules for wedding guests too? To ensure that you don't **inadvertently** (漫不经心地) commit a faux pas or do anything mistaken at a loved one's wedding, follow these simple rules.

RSVP promptly

Each invitation has an RSVP (abbreviation for French "Répondez s'il vous plaît", meaning "Reply, if you please") date. Because an accurate count is needed well before the date of the wedding, it wouldn't do to respond late, even if you don't plan to attend. Failure to respond in a timely manner is considered rude and disrespectful.

There are other things to note on the invitation. For instance, if you're allowed to bring a guest, this will be indicated as "and guest" next to your name on the invite. If this isn't indicated, you should assume the host is requesting only the honor of your presence and not that of your guest. It's very bad mannered to show up at the wedding, guests in two, when you didn't RSVP for two people. Bringing unexpected guests is very impolite. This includes your children or other relatives! This means the caterer will have to scramble to make sure they have enough meals, and the host will have to pay for that extra meal after the reception. In addition, if children are invited, this too will be noted on the invitation, either as "and family" next to your name on the envelope, or inside the invitation where children's names will be notated. If this isn't the case, assume you'll need to hire a baby sitter.

Send a gift/card in a proper way

It is customary to purchase a gift for the bride and groom, and a good price to spend on a wedding gift is between fifty dollars and a thousand dollars, depending on your relationship to the happy couple. But you don't have to bring the gift to the wedding with you. In many instances, gifts at the actual wedding are difficult to transport from the reception site back to the couple's home. If you are unable to attend the wedding, it's still proper etiquette to send a gift. Technically, a guest has one year to send a gift, but keeping the new couple waiting for the gift too long is awkward for all involved. Find the middle ground and be sure to give the couple a card on their wedding day. Follow up promptly with a gift, whether you deliver it in person or have it sent to their home.

Dress appropriately for the occasion
The invitation will usually specify the attire expected: informal, semiformal, or very formal. If it is not indicated on the invitation, contact a family member and ask. Dressing appropriately shows respect for the occasion and will keep you from feeling uncomfortable and out-of-place. Men seldom go wrong with a dark three-piece suit, although a very formal (black tie) wedding requires a **tuxedo** (无尾礼服), and at an informal wedding you might get by with a dress shirt and **slacks** (松身裤). Women should wear knee-length dresses for informal or semiformal ceremonies, and floor-length gowns for very formal ceremonies. You should save black for funerals. Wearing it to weddings is too **morbid** (可怕的). And red is too flashy to wear to weddings. Don't upstage the bride—no white or **sequins** (闪光金属片), which is considered "stealing the scene" from the bride; and no bare shoulders if the ceremony is held in a house of worship. Wear a jacket or wrap over your shoulders and remove it for the reception. Wearing an above the knee skirt or dress is fine as long as you have the legs for it. It's okay for women to wear pants. Do not wear jeans, shorts, sandals, sneakers, or caps unless the dress is "casual."

Arrive early to the ceremony
On the day of the wedding, don't be late. The last thing the happy couple wants is to have their wedding vows interrupted by the sound of heels walking down the aisle. If you are **tardy** (迟到的), and the procession is going on, stand at the rear of the wedding location and watch from afar, waiting until the bride reaches the altar to enter and find a seat.

Make your children on their best behavior
If children are invited, please see to it that they remain on their best behavior throughout. Not only is it annoying for the other wedding guests to put up with crying, laughing, playing and **admonishments** (告诫) in hushed tones, but it's disrespectful to the bride and groom. If your children insist on being noisy and distracting, you should take them out.

Don't take photographs during the ceremony
Even though we always see wedding guests **snapping away** (咔嚓拍照) during the ceremony, in reality it's considered bad manners to take pictures. Leave that to the professionals and respect the sanctity of the ritual in front of you. The photographer has copies you might want to purchase, or you can wait until after the ceremony is over. You can also take all the pictures you want at the reception.

Follow the seating charts and socialize
The wedding reception is usually held an hour or two after the ceremony, unless the reception and ceremony take place in the same location. In many cases, a cocktail hour is planned so guests can mingle while photographs and other wedding issues are taken care of. If there's a big gap between

the time the ceremony ends and the time you have to arrive at the reception, it's up to you to entertain yourself. Some people like to go to their homes or homes of other wedding guests to rest and freshen up before the festivities begin.

At the reception, look for place cards or a seating chart. You may not know the people who are at your table, but please don't complain to the couple or the family that you want to sit somewhere else. This is their day to celebrate, not to **indulge**（放任，纵容）**whiny**（爱抱怨的）guests! The seating arrangements are made with the consideration that table mates may enjoy each other. Introduce yourself and try to have a good time where you are. At the buffet table, be considerate of the other guests and do not load your plate up with food, and drink alcohol in moderation to avoid embarrassing yourself and the newly married couple. The home video may be **hilarious**（欢闹的）on TV, but it's doubtful that the bride and groom will appreciate your **antics**（滑稽举止）.

Exercises

Choose the best answer to each question.

1. With a wedding invitation, you are expected to _____.
   A. respond to the invitation timely whether you plan to attend or not
   B. not to respond to the invitation if you don't plan to attend
   C. bring a guest to the wedding to give the bride and groom a surprise
   D. show up alone at the wedding even though the invitation is indicated "and guest"

2. Which is TRUE regarding giving a wedding gift?
   A. The more intimate you are with the couple, the more expensive the gift you purchase.
   B. It's proper etiquette to send the gift to the couple a year after the wedding.
   C. Make sure to bring the gift and give it to the couple at the actual wedding.
   D. It's proper etiquette to send a gift to the couple even if you cannot attend the wedding.

3. Dressing properly includes the following EXCEPT that _____.
   A. guests do not wear red to weddings
   B. guests dress in the attire expected in the invitation
   C. men never attend the wedding with a dark three-piece suit
   D. women wear floor-length gowns for formal ceremonies

4. Which of the following is appropriate for a wedding guest?
   A. Stand outside the wedding location if you are late.
   B. Admonish your children's improper behavior repeatedly in hushed tones.
   C. Take as many pictures as possible for the bride and groom during the wedding.
   D. Accept the seating arrangements even though you do not know the people at your table.

5. It's acceptable to _____.

    A. embarrass yourself to amuse the couple and the guests

    B. take food and drink alcohol moderately at the buffet

    C. introduce yourself to everyone at the party

    D. take care of other guests and load their plate up with food

Passage 2

Wedding Toast and Other Guest Etiquette

A wedding is one of the most important occasions in the life of an individual. If you are a close friend or family member of the bride or the groom, such as the best man or the bridesmaid, it is expected of you to give a toast at their wedding and bless them with your good wishes.

● Make sure to complement the bride. It is sort of an "unspoken rule." However, you need to make sure that it is genuine, so that you do not end up looking like a liar in front of the guests. You can say something about her beauty, smile, the happiness that is reflecting from her face.

● Do not include topics that are **racy** (猥亵的) or embarrassing. How you had a great time on a bachelor trip to Hawaii or how you girls went **drooling** (迷恋地看) over every guy you saw on a vacation to Rio de Janeiro is something that no couple would want to hear about on their wedding day.

● Any talk about the ex-girlfriends, ex-boyfriends, or ex-spouses of the couple is definitely something that is not to be mentioned in a wedding toast. Also out of bounds are statements about the cost of the wedding, wedding gifts, future plans of the couple or their honeymoon trip.

● Make sure to thank the hosts, be it the bride's family or the newly wedded couple, for the excellent party. Express your delight for their hospitality as well as their good taste. This is something very important, which most people forget to do.

● Close your wedding toast on a high and hopeful note. Express your best wishes for the couple to have a happy, healthy and prosperous future. Ask everybody present at the party to join you in the wedding toast, lift your champagne glass, and say, "To (name of bride) and (name of groom)."

● It is a wedding toast and not a speech, though quite similar. Ensure that it does not stretch on for more than 5 minutes.

● While giving the toast, always focus on the couple. Keep your eyes fixed on them, while glancing at the guests occasionally.

- Avoid talking about your own marriage or relationship. It is the time to convey your best wishes for the couple.

- Do not get drunk. If you want to **gulp down** (畅饮) a number of drinks, at least wait till you have given the wedding toast.

- The bride and groom get the honor of the first dance. It may be at the beginning of the reception or later on, and once they have had their dance, feel free to cut loose!

- Before making your exit, be sure to find a member of the family, or the married couple if they are still there, and thank them for a wonderful time.

- The most important rule of attending a wedding is to enjoy the day. The bride and groom planned this special day in celebration of a joyous affair and took their guests' comfort and entertainment into heavy consideration. Be respectful, be polite and be a good guest.

Exercises

Choose the best answer to each question.

1. _____ is NOT expected to give a toast to the couple at their wedding.
    A. The best man
    B. The groom's brother
    C. The bride's father
    D. The wedding host

2. When giving a toast at a wedding, it is appropriate to _____.
    A. talk only about the groom but not the bride
    B. mention the smile on the bride's face
    C. talk about your own marriage
    D. ask the groom not to lie to the bride

3. The toast at the wedding could include topics like _____.
    A. your appreciation for the excellent wedding party
    B. what a great time you had on a bachelor trip
    C. a comparison between the ex-girlfriend and the bride
    D. what a unique honeymoon trip the couple will enjoy

4. An appropriate wedding toast _____.
    A. should be a very long and rich speech
    B. includes interesting stories of your marriage

C. thanks the caterer first for the excellent party

D. should be closed on a high and hopeful note

5. Which of following statements is TRUE of "Be respectful, be polite, and be a good guest"?

   A. It's fine to get drunk since it shows that you are making good wishes for the couple.

   B. Thank the couple or one of their family members before making your exit.

   C. Only the best man and bridesmaid get the honor of the first dance with the bride at the wedding ceremony.

   D. The most important thing for a guest at a wedding is to make the best toast to the new couple.

SECTION 6   CULTURAL EXPLORATION

In this section, you will learn Chinese etiquette from the cultural perspective.

Task 1   Understanding Chinese etiquette in ancient poems or famous quotes

Read and study the following ancient Chinese poem related to wedding ceremony in English and then find out its original Chinese version. What message is being conveyed in this poem?

Peach Blossoms Beam

By Anonymity

Translated by Xu Yuanchong

The peach tree beams so red,
How brilliant are its flowers!
The maiden's getting wed,
Good for the nuptial bowers.

The peach tree beams so red,
How abundant its fruits!
The maiden's getting wed,
Good as family's root.

The peach tree beams so red,
Its leaves are manifold.
The maiden's getting wed,
Good for the whole household.

_____

Unit 9　Attending a Wedding Ceremony

作者_____
译者_____

_____
_____
_____
_____
_____
_____
_____
_____
_____
_____

Task 2　Learning Chinese traditions related to the etiquette of this unit

Read the following introduction to Chinese wedding dress traditions on the wedding day and identify the major cultural points included in the passage. Then pick out some key words or cultural expressions that help you remember and understand the major points.

> In China, the colors and ornamentations of wedding dresses are all Chinese-style blessings based on different cultural traditions.
>
> According to He Yang, director of the National Costume Museum, "Clothing presents an image in your eyes and gives you a feeling. For example, the color red gives you a festive feeling, and both gold and red create a festive and affluent atmosphere, so the two colors are indispensable for a wedding."
>
> Besides color, pattern is also very important, as it can help create associations. The pattern of flower bouquets on a brocade fabric symbolizes wonderful things. Blessings from Chinese people for newlyweds have been hidden secretly in the patterns of the wedding clothing. "The most commonly used pattern during the wedding is the combination of a dragon and a phoenix," according to Zhong Mantian, visiting professor at the Beijing Institute of Fashion Technology. "Some patterns of plants are also used. For example, peony flowers are a symbol of luxury. Lotuses on the wedding dress show the innocence of the new wives since lotuses live in the silt but are not imbrued. Moreover, it is also a

symbol of many children and many blessings as when lotuses blossom, they bear seed pods with many seeds."

The guests at a Chinese wedding won't wear red because that's the privilege of the couple. Also, white and black are not suitable for a wedding. These colors are often worn at Chinese funerals and signify death and mourning. The best colors for a Chinese wedding are warm soft colors like purple, pink, and peach—they all symbolize new life and happiness. Gold is also a popular color in Chinese culture. All these hues are acceptable as they are thought to bring good luck to the newlyweds.

In each period of time, clothing reflects characteristics of that time. Changes in the scenes of people's lives can have a lot of influence on the changes in our clothing. There is a fundamental point when wearing these garments and it is to become more beautiful, present better taste, and appear to be richer, more charismatic and different. These goals will never change. Chinese wedding clothing has been constantly changing throughout history, but the essence of it has not changed; it is the evidence of the blood connection between generations of Chinese people, and the inheritance of Chinese civilization.

1. Major cultural points in the story:

   (1) _____
   (2) _____
   (3) _____
   (4) _____
   (5) _____

2. Major words or cultural expressions in the story:

   (1) Para. 1 _____
   (2) Para. 2 _____
   (3) Para. 3 _____
   (4) Para. 4 _____
   (5) Para. 5 _____

3. What interesting stories about traditions or manners in attending a wedding ceremony would you like to share with your classmates?

Unit 10

Touring Abroad and Leisure Time

You will learn in this unit
☐ concert etiquette
☐ sports spectator etiquette
☐ understanding tip culture
☐ behaving appropriately in public places

SECTION 1 INTRODUCTION

🎧 Listen to the following passage and fill in the blanks.

Obeying the 1._____ of a country is common sense for modern people. However, it sometimes takes more than that common sense to become a 2._____ when people 3._____. When touring another country people are something of a 4._____ their home country. So it's always a good idea to get familiarized with the ways and customs of the local people before getting there. For example, in countries like America, and the UK in the West and Thailand in the East, people tip the service clerks while people don't do that in countries like Australia. Tipping culture 5._____ in many Western countries and can also be found in some of the South-eastern Asian countries where neglecting the tip culture could bring about an 6._____ situation for Australian tourists. Another example is that Italian people prefer to enjoy 7._____. However, they may encounter 8._____ if they bring the custom of "happy noise" to a country where quietness is regarded as 9._____. Therefore, learning and respecting local customs would definitely benefit cross-culture tourists. Wherever you are a tourist, it is always advisable to keep in your mind: 10._____.

SECTION 2 CHECK YOUR MANNERS

Read the following statements and mark T for the true statements and F for the false statements. Provide corrections for the false ones.

___ 1. It is acceptable for spectators to applaud and acclaim loudly whenever they feel excited during a sports game.

___ 2. In the theater one should never leave while the actors are on the stage or while music is being played.

___ 3. Preventable movements such as leaning to whisper to your neighbor, or large movements such as stretching, are completely unacceptable during a song.

___ 4. During a performance in the theater, you should not eat, drink, or smoke. If you are suffering from a cough, be discreet when unwrapping and sucking a cough drop, but any other eating should be saved for intermissions.

___ 5. Don't talk loudly in public places especially during a performance.

___ 6. If you want to take photos, you should ask for permission before the event.

___ 7. Keep your voice low, especially when you are in museum or art gallery.
___ 8. In Western countries, you should give tips to whoever provides you with service.
___ 9. The "first custom" in the international society is "guest first."
___ 10. You will probably not feel comfortable at a classical concert if you dress in a respectful manner.

SECTION 3 PRACTICE

In this section, proper etiquette will be learned through different tasks.

Task 1 Learning to tip

Complete the dialogues with the words or expressions given in the box, and learn how people should tip appropriately abroad.

Conversation 1

| disagree | the bill | over-tipped | disappointed |
| good service | tip | twenty-five percent | |

(Two Australian tourists are unpacking in their San Diego hotel room.)

Susan: Did you tip the bellboy?
Tom: Yes, but I don't think it was enough. He looked 1._____. I gave him three dollars.
Susan: That sounds about right to me, fifty cents a bag. If they think you don't know any better, they'll try to get more.
Tom: I definitely think we 2._____ the cab driver. The fare was twenty dollars, and you gave him a five-dollar tip. That's 3._____ of the total?! Too much!
Susan: I 4._____. He was polite and informative and he drove smoothly. One should reward 5._____.

(Later in the hotel dining room)

Tom: I'll sign for dinner and charge it to your room. Let's see. The bill is one hundred dollars. That seems reasonable. How much 6._____ should I leave?
Susan: Remember last month when we were in Europe. Maybe Californians use that same system: they add the waiter or waitress into 7._____, so you don't have to leave anything extra.

Conversation 2

offensive	the bill	low	good service
pick up	the service	a good tip	how much to pay
tips	wages	custom	fifteen percent

(Lily and her American friend Martin are having dinner in a restaurant.)

Lily: Can I at least help you pay a little?
Martin: If you really want to, I guess you could 1._____ the tip.
Lily: OK. How much should that be?
Martin: You don't tip in your country?
Lily: No, not at all, so I have no idea 2._____.
Martin: In restaurants, fifteen percent of 3._____ is considered pretty standard.
Lily: What if 4._____ is really bad?
Martin: You didn't like your server?
Lily: Oh, she was fine. I was just wondering.
Martin: The lowest you can get away with without being really 5._____ is ten percent. And twenty percent is considered 6._____.
Lily: Why do people feel obligated to tip? Shouldn't a server's 7._____ be enough?
Martin: Servers depend on 8._____ to survive. Restaurant owners know that, so their wages are 9._____.
Lily: But why do people pay them?
Martin: It's a 10._____. Plus, it encourages 11._____. Servers know they'll earn more for better service.
Lily: That makes sense. 12._____ of eighty dollars is … eight plus four …
Martin: You are good at math.

Task 2 Making a custom-comparison among countries

The following lists are some customs in Western countries. Compare them and find out the differences. What kind of problems may these differences cause when one is touring abroad? Work in groups, and act out a role-play to show the problems.

1. The United Kingdom: Don't bargain

Don't bargain in Britain when you go shopping. British people rarely bargain, because it is against the law. However, if you visit a market towards the end of the day, you can sometimes bargain with the stall-holder for fruit and vegetables.

2. Germany: Don't give presents or say "Happy birthday!" before one's birthday.
According to German customs, birthdays should not be congratulated in advance.

3. America and some other Western countries: Don't make an appointment on Friday 13th.
Judas, one **disciple** (信徒, 徒弟) of Jesus, betrayed Jesus for thirty silver coins and as a result Jesus died on a cross. Da Vinci's famous painting *The Last Supper* depicts Jesus and his disciples having dinner before the betrayal. In the Painting, the thirteenth person is the traitor Judas and the day on which Jesus died was a Friday.

Task 3 Group discussion

Read the following story, and then discuss in small groups how the spectators should behave when watching sports games.

> A visible increase in the interest in sports and outdoor activities over the last decade has changed the dynamics of the outbound Chinese tourism market and as a result, more Chinese travelers plan overseas holidays in line with opportunities to watch or take part in high-profile sporting events. Sport-related tourism has emerged as a significant element of global tourism. In the UK, this has been really noticeable in the Premier League, where more and more Chinese fans are going to watch soccer teams that have developed big followings in China.
>
> "The affluent young Chinese outbound traveler is very discerning, very well educated and very experience-driven," said James Kenny, Tourism Ireland's China manager. "They are leading the way in setting new trends and sports-related tourism is one of those trends."

SECTION 4 CASE STUDY

Read the following cases and do each case study in small groups. The questions in "Critical thinking" after each case are aimed to help with finding the story background, the problem itself, the etiquette involved, and the cultural differences behind the etiquette. Remember to provide possible solutions to the problem in each case.

Case 1

The Musician's Sad Tears

An art school was holding a classical concert in their concert hall. On the stage was Professor Audrey, who was from the French National Music School. She has held more than 200 concerts around the world and the audiences who have attended her concerts are all moved by her superb performances. On this occasion, however, just as the concert began, tears welled up in her eyes causing the concert to be interrupted. Why? Most of the audience watching the performance were children with their parents. The parents desired to cultivate their children's interest in classical music. But these children were too young and immature to enjoy Audrey's elegant performance. They could not sit still. They climbed up and down, yelled loudly and created chaos. The parents did not seem to care about their children's misbehavior as they added to the noisy environment by constantly using their mobile phones.

Professor Audrey could no longer stand the noise and she had to leave the stage with tears of sadness in her eyes.

Critical thinking

1. Retell the case in 3–4 sentences using the expressions in the box.

hold an elegant concert	superb	burst into tears
develop one's interest	yell	immature

2. If you attended Professor Audrey's concert, how would you behave well?

3. The audience in some countries would applaud or cheer loudly when watching traditional performances while those from other cultures would keep quiet most of the time during the performance (e.g. attending concerts). Could you think of some examples? Why do you think there are such differences?

Case 2

Who Was Wrong?

(A hotel room in Phoenix, Arizona, 7 p.m. A weary traveler, recently off a 12-hour flight from a South-eastern Asian country, has just eaten in the hotel restaurant and is about to get into bed.)

Caller: Hi, Mr. Durante. This is Brad here, your waiter for this evening.

Me: (puzzled but friendly) Oh, hi, Brad.

Brad: I was just calling to check that you enjoyed your meal this evening.

Me: Well, cheers for asking, Brad. It was fine.

Brad: Only, I guess you being tired and all, you forgot to express your appreciation in the customary way…

Like a lemon I get dressed, go downstairs and hand Brad a five dollar note. The recollection of this episode has tortured me ever since. Yes, I know that Brad gets paid diddly-squat and like all American waiters relies on tips. I realized I had screwed up. But I was already in my pajamas, for God's sake.

Critical thinking

1. Retell the case in 2–3 sentences using the expressions in the box.

weary	flight	puzzle	recollection	torture

2. Why does Brad come to see Mr. Durante? Do you think what Brad does is acceptable?

Case 3

Tennis Etiquette—Where Has It Gone?

During this year's tournament, I was struck by the number of attendees who were infants and toddlers. While I was watching Tommy Haas' match on one of the outside courts, I was stunned to see a mother carrying two toddlers—one on her back and another slung across her chest. Thankfully for Tommy and the rest of us sitting on the small, intimate court that it was naptime for those little ones. But, what about the ones who wail, scream and cry during match play when their parents are sitting so close to the court? Kids under a minimum age are not allowed to attend live concerts and Broadway performances—both are also live events. So, why are they allowed onto the grounds? I am not shutting kids out of the game, but would mind boosting attendance at Arthur Ashe's Kids Day! It is no secret that US tennis is losing its competitive edge. So, are we starting these kids young by bringing them to the courts while they are still in diapers?

And, what about the cell phones that ring during match play? And, the ensuing conversations that take place during match play! Are you joking? Should an announcement be made to turn these devices off before or after the rules of the challenge system are detailed?

How about those fans strolling around the stands when a player is in the middle of a first serve? Well, some of those fans look like they should stroll more, but around the track and not around Arthur Ashe Stadium Court. Has waiting for a changeover become a pastime like the all-white tennis garb that was clad by players of yesteryear? I'd like to bring both of those pastimes back, actually! After such poor etiquette from that the questioned, I did not dare to ask another fan why that hot dog and beer were so necessary at that very moment rather than in a mere ten or fifteen minutes. Maybe the ushers can help us out on this front. Please do a better job keeping the fans in their seats (or in the waiting areas) during match play. If that is not possible, please direct these people to CitiField across the boardwalk. Maybe they are better suited to sit over there.

Critical thinking

1. Retell the case in 3–4 sentences using the expressions in the box.

tournament	struck	attendees	infants
stroll around	during match play		

2. What poor etiquette is mentioned by the author in this case? How can you be a well-behaved sports spectator?

SECTION 5   READING FOR ETIQUETTE TIPS

Read the following passages and finish the exercises after each of the texts.

Passage 1

Concert Hall Etiquette

Good etiquette in any social situation has one basic purpose: to show consideration for others. When applied to the concert situation, good etiquette is required so that everyone in the hall is allowed to fully enjoy what they came for—to share a musical experience. Acceptable behavior in a concert hall is not the same as acceptable behavior at a sporting event or rock concert, where good-natured **rowdiness** (吵闹) is often considered to be part of the fun. At a conventional concert, the focus should be on what is happening on stage, not what is happening in the audience.

Common sense, then, should tell us that unacceptable concert behavior includes doing anything that focuses the attention of the performers or fellow **concert-goers** (常去听演唱会的人) on you, rather than on the music that is being presented on stage. This is a very general rule, covering all kinds of poor etiquette habits. The following are just a few guidelines that should help you **differentiate** (区分 ; 区别) between proper etiquette and **obnoxious** (讨厌的), distracting behavior.

Entering and exiting the auditorium

You should make every attempt to arrive at a concert a few minutes early, so that you can find your seat and be settled before the performance starts. Once you take your seat, plan on staying there until the entire concert is over (unless there is an official intermission). Use the restroom before the performance starts!

There may be circumstances where it is absolutely not possible for you to stay for the entire concert. If this is the case, you may be allowed to enter or leave the auditorium between songs. You must do this as quickly and quietly as possible, to minimize the distraction to others. You should never be moving around the auditorium while a group is performing on stage. If you don't have time to slip quietly into your seat before the next song begins, then wait outside for the next break.

The only acceptable reason for leaving the auditorium during a song is if your presence in the auditorium will be more disruptive than your walking out (for instance, if you are suddenly caught in an uncontrollable coughing fit). If this happens, get out as quickly as possible, and don't come back until your problem is under control.

Cell phones and pagers

If you must carry one of these devices into a concert, please be sure it is turned off. A ringing phone or pager can ruin the experience for everyone in the room.

Talking and fidgeting (坐立不安)

Many people don't seem to realize how much every little movement they make can distract the people around them. A movement as subtle as turning your head can be enough to distract people for several rows behind you. Sure, you will probably need to adjust your position from time to time to remain comfortable. For the sake of everyone around you, though, you should try to keep such adjustments to a minimum.

Preventable movements such as leaning to whisper to your neighbor, or large movements such as stretching, are completely unacceptable during a song. If you are over the age of five, there is no reason why you shouldn't be able to hold off on such movements until the song is over.

There is also no good reason to make distracting noises while the music is playing. Talking, humming, playing with keys, rustling your **program** (节目单)—these are all unacceptable and distracting behaviors. Laughing is appropriate when the performance is supposed to be funny. Laughing is not appropriate if something unintentionally funny happens on stage, or if someone else in the audience does something distracting.

Do not bring work into the concert with you. You are there to listen to the music—not to write, read, etc. Anything you do, other than sitting quietly and listening to the music, prevents others from enjoying the performance.

Have a sore throat or cough? Many a concert moment has been ruined by a member of the audience slowly unwrapping a cough drop during a song. Try to plan ahead: if you have been having problems with coughing, put a cough drop in your mouth before the concert starts, and try to only unwrap them between songs from then on. If you must put one in your mouth during a song, unwrap it quickly (face it—it can't be done quietly, so just yank the thing out of there as fast as you can) and be done with it. If you think you may have a coughing fit, try to sit near an exit, so you won't have far to go if you need to leave quickly.

Applause

It is wonderful when students in an audience want to support their classmates by showing enthusiasm before and after a group performs. The appropriate way to show your appreciation for a performance and to show your support for friends as they are walking onto the stage is to clap.

Screaming, catcalling, yelling out people's names, and other loud vocal noises only serve to call attention to you, and are not acceptable in a conventional concert situation. This sort of **rowdy** (吵闹的) behavior can quickly get out of hand, and can really **detract** (消减) from the enjoyment of people who don't appreciate loud, screaming crowds. Again, this is a difference between the concert hall setting and a basketball game or rock event. Screaming will not be acceptable at any performance at a major concert hall, and it is not acceptable at a high school music concert, either.

Food and drinks

A concert hall is not a movie theatre. You should never bring food or drinks into a concert. If you have a legitimate health concern, where you must keep your throat lubricated, try to keep a hard candy or cough drop in your mouth (see cough drop advice under "Talking and Fidgeting," above). If you are so sick that you can't get through an entire concert without a drink of water, maybe you should stay home and not spread your illness to the rest of the audience.

Exercises

Choose the best answer to each question.

1. What is usually considered as the basic purpose of good etiquette in any social situation?
    A. To show consideration for others.
    B. To appreciate others' consideration.
    C. To enjoy oneself.
    D. To entertain others.
2. Which of the following statements is true about acceptable concert behavior?
    A. Good-natured rowdiness is often considered to be part of the fun.
    B. You can scream, catcall and yell out people's names to show you are really enjoying the concert.
    C. Do anything that focuses the attention of the performers or fellow concert-goers on you, rather than on the music that is being presented on stage.
    D. You should leave the auditorium if you are caught in a sudden uncontrollable coughing fit.
3. What is the only acceptable reason for leaving the auditorium during a song?
    A. You have to use the restroom.
    B. Your presence in the auditorium is more disruptive than walking out.
    C. You don't like the performance on the stage.
    D. You have to receive a phone call.
4. Which of the following is appropriate to show your appreciation for a concert?
    A. To dance to the music.
    B. To wave to the performer(s) on the stage.

C. To clap.

D. To cheer loudly.

5. At a concert hall, what is acceptable behavior concerning food and drinks?

A. You should never bring food or drinks into a concert.

B. You should not have a hard candy or cough drop in your mouth in any situation.

C. You should bring some water if you are sick.

D. You should slowly unwrap a cough drop during a song.

Passage 2

Tipping Etiquette in Western Countries

While you may think the cost of service is included in the food, it isn't. Tipping is **ingrained** (根深蒂固) into numerous cultures, and if you try to get away without tipping, you'll only look foolish and rude. Tipping is a way to show your appreciation for good or exceptional service.

Tipping by geography

Australia

Tipping in Australia is basically non-existent.

Canada

Most service staff in Canada expect something in the 10%–20% tip range, depending on what city, if it's French or English Canada, and the level of service. Tipping is expected for restaurants, bars, food delivery and taxis. You should not try to tip the police, especially the Royal Canadian Mountain Police—they will not appreciate it. 15% is a good tip in a restaurant. In Montreal, tips for a good meal at a good restaurant with good service should be more. In most of English Canada, you would find it a lot harder to have the same experience, and anyway would not be expected to tip as much.

On the other hand, you should not tip if service is bad. If the service is really bad, leave a nickel, and they should get the message. There is no excuse for bad service—it's so easy to give! And if you work in the service industry, the little effort can gain you a personal reward-tip!

France

In France, in restaurants, though not at bars, service must be included by law in the price. It is usually about 15% or so.

Germany

Tipping seems strange to many Germans. The people you expect to tip (loo attendants for example) have a fixed price but tipping hairdressers and the like may seem **akin to** (类似) starting a revolution.

I almost never tip taxi drivers, since mostly they don't even open the door for me. But I do leave a **pressie** (赠品) for the bin men on the first collection after Christmas. Despite my nagging suspicion, they earn more than me.

New Zealand

Don't tip. Ever. You don't have to. People will generally be nice to you as long as you don't treat them like your personal slave. Service is almost always included, as is the sales tax, so the price you see is the price you are charged. The only exceptions are:

- exceptionally good service
- if the menu says "Service not Included" (rare)
- telling the taxi driver to keep the change so he doesn't have to **fumble** (摸索) around for 35 cents

Conversely, New Zealanders (and Australians too) are notoriously bad tippers, and consequently get bad service sometimes in other countries.

United Kingdom

All British people know this: you do not tip at the bar in a pub. If you are impressed with the **barkeep**'s (酒吧间侍者) service, you can offer to buy them a drink. Such an offer will be genuinely appreciated, even though it may not be accepted. If it is, the barkeep might take the tip in the form of cash to have one (a drink) later. This will generally be for half a pint of beer, or a small measure of spirits—you would not expect them to take for a larger drink unless you specifically asked them to.

It seems to be a grey area whether to tip for meals served in a pub. Generally, you have to decide whether a particular establishment is a pub that serves food (don't tip) or a restaurant with a bar (do tip).

United States

Restaurants in the USA usually call for a 15%–20% tip. However, if your server is a complete jerk, you aren't expected to give them a dime of your pocket-money. Of course, you may have the misfortune of going to a restaurant that automatically includes a 15% tip in the check, but for all those US males out there who pull out their little calculators every time they receive the bill, having the tip already indicated for them can save a lot of embarrassment.

In pubs, you are expected to put a dollar or two into the pot at the bar. However, since you usually pay only at the end (rather than for each drink as you go), this does not get too expensive!

In most states of the US the tax is around 7%–8%, so you just tip twice the tax—a little more or less depending on the service you got. However, some people just don't understand what the big deal is with figuring out what 15% of the total is … You just take ten percent of the total, divide that by two, and then find the sum of both figures!

Tipping in different public places

Tipping etiquette in restaurants

The standard tip is 15%–20%, depending on the service. A few years ago, 15% was considered generous, but now it's a sign that you found their customer service merely acceptable. Excellent service deserves more, particularly as tips in good restaurants are shared with busboys.

Tipping in hotels and airports

Generally, tipping in airports and on arrival at your hotel is reserved for the bag handlers. Porters should get one to two dollars per bag, or more if they're particularly heavy.

At the hotel, tip the maid daily as a different person may be cleaning your room on different days. Again, good customer service earns more, with two to three dollars for great service and a dollar a day for lower-level service. Remember to tip the valet parking attendant and the attendants at the pool if they're fetching deck chairs and towels. Room service tipping is the same as restaurant service at 15%–20%.

No tipping necessary

In some establishments, such as bed and breakfasts or small restaurants where the owner serves your meal, no tip is expected and it may even be prohibited. Large grocery store chains don't allow their employees to accept tips for taking groceries to your car. In foreign countries, enquire before tipping.

In some establishments the service charge is added to the bill and no additional tipping is expected. For knock-your-socks-off exceptional service, though, you're free to leave extra. If you're not sure whether service is included, ask. Many US restaurants add 15% for service when your party is relatively large.

Tipping tour guides, bus drivers, and taxi drivers overseas

You should plan to tip your tour guide 15%–20% of the cost of the tour. If your hotel provides the tour, tip them in foreign currency equivalent to about three or four US dollars a day. Taxi drivers should receive 15% of the fare as a tip, and up to 20% if they hold your door open, help you with baggage or answer questions. Bus drivers who handle baggage should be tipped like skycaps and **bellboys** (行李员；服务生).

Unit 10 Touring Abroad and Leisure Time

Exercises

Choose the best answer to each question.

1. In Canada, you should not tip if you _____.
   A. take a taxi
   B. are not satisfied with the service
   C. go to the hairdresser's
   D. don't like the police

2. You would not tip in New Zealand when _____.
   A. the menu says "Service not Included"
   B. you tell the taxi driver to keep the change
   C. you receive exceptionally good service
   D. the attendants in hotels fetch deck chairs and towels for you

3. Which of the following statements is true?
   A. Tipping is very common in Australia.
   B. In France, service must be included in the price at bars.
   C. You should tip at the bar in a pub in UK.
   D. Service is almost always included, as is the sales tax in New Zealand.

4. Restaurants in the USA usually call for a _____ tip unless the service is really bad.
   A. 15%–20%
   B. 10%–20%
   C. 7%–8%
   D. fixed

5. In some establishments, such as bed and breakfasts or small restaurants where the owner serves your meal, _____.
   A. you should always leave extra
   B. tipping twice the tax is appropriate
   C. no tipping is expected and it may even be prohibited
   D. it seems to be a grey area whether to tip or not

Passage 3

Staying in a Hotel and Visiting a Museum Abroad

Hotel etiquette: hotel rooms and your comfort

Hotel rooms are supposed to be your home away from home, so hoteliers are interested in making you feel comfortable and welcome. Being an appreciative guest involves more than just leaving the hotel maid a good tip.

Hotel owners have many stories about guests who have left their rooms in **deplorable** (糟透的) conditions, particularly bathrooms. While you are a paying customer, it's common courtesy to leave your room in a decent condition. Otherwise, you will leave your hosts with the impression that everyone from your state or country of origin is a born **slob** (粗俗汉).

Many hotels are committed to the preservation of natural resources, such as the water and electricity needed to launder towels that may have been used to wipe clean bodies only once. If you want your towels replaced, leave them on the floor, otherwise, hang them on towel bars, hooks and shower curtain bars.

Hotel rooms have trash **receptacles** (容器) in the bathroom and sleeping area for your use. If you have more trash than the small receptacles can hold, use plastic bags or call housekeeping. Don't leave trash in the public areas.

If you're traveling on hot summer days, you'll be tempted to fill your cooler from the ice machines. Clearly, the icemaker can't produce that much ice for each guest. As a courtesy to other hotel guests, stop at a convenience store or service station and spend a few bucks on a bag of ice.

If you're staying in a small inn or a bed-and-breakfast, be aware that you're all but living in someone's home. Respect the quiet hours and make an extra effort to keep things tidy.

If your neighbors are noisy or **imposing** (不合理的要求) on you in some way, don't get steamed up and start banging on walls. Instead, call the front desk and ask them to handle the matter.

If your stay was less than comfortable, leave a note or speak quietly to the manager about the problem. Remember that in many foreign cultures, loud complaints are considered rude. Don't expect a **reimbursement** (退还 ; 赔偿). There's a chance that your expectations were too high.

Museum etiquette: how to behave when visiting an art museum
Museums are great places to visit in order for people to appreciate art, history, science, innovation, etc. Museums are places where you can explore and learn about the past, present, and the future. Every museum has its own set of rules, oftentimes you find them in the **brochures** (小册子) or pamphlets, and some are posted by the entrance where every visitor can see. Aside from that, there are museum representatives and guides that would announce the rules before proceeding to let you in.

Museum etiquette 1: eating and drinking
When you go to a museum, you will be asked not to bring any food and/or drink. It is best that you schedule a museum visit after you have already had a meal, this way you do not have to

worry about getting hungry. Occasionally, they will allow you to chew gum or a small candy, if they do allow this make sure that you do not blow your bubble gum close to the art pieces. There are certain museums, for fear of any candy droppings or possible accidents with bubble gum mess, that would not even allow you to have these so it is always better to ask for permission first.

Museum etiquette 2: smoking

Smoking is not allowed inside the museum. If you must smoke, do it outside of the building. Smoking is generally not allowed inside public establishment in the United States because of health hazards. In museums however, it is not only the health hazards that are being considered when banning smoking, but the effect of smoke on the museum pieces. Smoke deposits can damage museum pieces, especially paintings and other rare artifacts.

Other etiquette in the museum

• Speak in a quiet voice in order not to disturb other visitors. Can you imagine sitting in front of your favorite piece of art for the first time only to hear some guy **yakking** (喋喋不休地讲) into his cell phone?

• Be aware of other visitors. Often, other visitors are sitting back from a piece to observe it or even sketch it on paper, so as a courtesy, try not to stand in their way. Also, I've seen people run into someone because they were paying attention to the artwork and forgot to look in front of them. This can be detrimental in a sculpture gallery!

• If you must take a photograph, do NOT use a flash. Bright lights can be destructive to a painting. One or two shots of a painting might not seem like a big deal, but they add up over time. This is why most galleries usually use low lighting.

Exercises

Choose the best answer to each question.

1. Which of the following can be considered as an appropriate hotel etiquette?
    A. Respect the quiet hours and make an extra effort to keep things clean if you are staying in a small inn or a bed-and-breakfast.
    B. If you have more trash than the small receptacles can hold, leave the trash in the public areas.
    C. If your neighbors are too noisy, knock on their doors and tell them to be quiet.
    D. Complain to the manager and ask for a reimbursement if your stay was less than comfortable.

2. When you visit an art museum, you should _____.

   A. bring your own food and/or drink

   B. never take photographs

   C. not carry your cell phone with you

   D. read the rules on the brochures or pamphlets

3. Smoking is banned in museums because _____.

   A. other visitors don't like the smell

   B. it may damage museum pieces

   C. it may cause health hazards

   D. most artists have quitted smoking

4. _____ is acceptable in an art museum.

   A. Speaking in a library voice

   B. Making/receiving a phone call

   C. Running around

   D. Blowing your bubble gum

5. You should not use a flash when taking a photograph in a gallery because _____.

   A. using a flash may influence the quality of the photo

   B. other visitors may feel uncomfortable with bright lights

   C. bright lights can be destructive to a painting

   D. the noise of the flash may disturb other visitors

SECTION 6   CULTURAL EXPLORATION

In this section, you will learn Chinese etiquette from the cultural perspective.

Task 1   Understanding Chinese etiquette in ancient poems or famous quotes

Read and study the following ancient Chinese poem related to leisure time in English and then find out its original Chinese version. What message is being conveyed in this poem?

On Qiantang Lake in Spring

By Bai Juyi

Translated by Xu Yuanchong

West of Jia Pavilion and north of Lonely Hill,

Water brims level with the bank and clouds hang low.

Disputing for sunny trees, early orioles trill;

Pecking vernal mud in, young swallows come and go.

A riot of blooms begins to dazzle the eye;
Amid short grass the horse hoofs can barely be seen.
I love best the east of the lake under the sky;
The bank paved with white sand is shaded by willows green.

_____

作者_____
译者_____

_____
_____
_____
_____
_____
_____
_____

Task 2 Learning Chinese traditions related to the etiquette of this unit

Read the short passage about Cuju in China and identify the major cultural points included in the introduction to Cuju. Then pick out some key words or cultural expressions that help you remember and understand the major points.

> Cuju, also known as kickball, is a traditional sport in China. "Cu" means to kick, and "ju" is a kind of ball that was used in ancient China, usually made of leather and filled with feathers. The players use their feet to kick the ball into the goal. The goal is usually a net or a hole in the ground.
>
> Cuju is believed to have originated in China before the Warring Sates Period (476BC–221BC). It was not only a sport, but also a way of entertainment. It was often played in the royal court and was even used as a way to train soldiers and select people for the army. In the Han Dynasty, Cuju became very popular and thriving. It's recorded in *Book of Han* that Han Gaozu Liu Bang (the first emperor of the Han Dynasty), was a kickball lover and he even built the tremendous court named "Cu City" in the palace.
>
> Cuju was an important part of ancient Chinese culture, often appearing in poetry and literature. However, little is known about the competition rules of Cuju in the Han Dynasty.

> One can only learn it from the poem "An Inscription about Cuju" by Li You in the Eastern Han Dynasty:
>
> *A ball and a court, Yin and Yang on the theory is based.*
>
> *A net on each side of it, twelve doers of every team play.*
>
> *Long and plain the court is, people do it with certain rules.*
>
> *No care whoever the players are, air is theirs.*
>
> *Calm the player should be, and complaint is in no need.*
>
> *Rules of Cuju're serious, and the same of the country's charge.*
>
> From the poem we can learn that the ball was round, and the court was square. At each end of the court there was a net and there were 12 players in each of the two teams. The referees were required to be fair. Thus Cuju is almost the same as the modern game of football.

1. Major cultural points in the story:

    (1) _____

    (2) _____

    (3) _____

2. Major words or cultural expressions in the story:

    (1) Para. 1 _____

    (2) Para. 2 _____

    (3) Para. 3 _____

3. What interesting stories about football or other sports would you like to share with your classmates?

Bibliography

参考书目：

范莹, 等. 中外礼仪集萃. 上海：上海外语教育出版社, 1999.

博斯特. 礼仪：雕饰最优雅的你. 西安：陕西师范大学出版社, 2009.

高福进. 西方人的习俗礼仪及文化. 上海：上海辞书出版社, 2003.

浩瀚. 社交英语对答如流. 北京：旅游教育出版社, 2008.

欧玲, 等. 西方礼仪文化. 重庆：重庆大学出版社, 2008.

吴光华. 汉英大词典（第三版）. 上海：上海译文出版社, 2009.

许渊冲. 唐诗三百首（汉英对照）. 北京：高等教育出版社, 2000.

许渊冲. 许渊冲经典英译古代诗歌1000首：汉魏六朝诗. 北京：海豚出版社, 2013.

许渊冲. 许渊冲译李白诗选（汉英双语）. 北京：中译出版社, 2021.

许渊冲, 译. 论语（汉英对照）. 北京：五洲传播出版社, 2019.

许渊冲, 陆苏. 林深见鹿：美得窒息的唐诗（英汉对照）. 武汉：长江文艺出版社, 2020.

许渊冲, 许明. 许译中国经典诗文集——宋元明清诗选. 北京：五洲传播出版社, 2018.

许渊冲, 闫红. 燕燕于飞：美得窒息的诗经（英汉对照）. 武汉：长江文艺出版社, 2020.

杨伯峻, 等. 论语今译. 济南：齐鲁书社, 1993.

张国亮. 亮出最好的自己. 北京：中信出版社, 2008.

Irimiaş, E. Cultural Differences Reconciled by Business Etiquette. *Lingua. B. Culture & Civilization*, 2009, 8, 69–79.

参考网站：

http://academia.stackexchange.com

https://www.bilibili.com

http://www.chinadaily.com.cn

https://ctext.org

https://www.diffordsguide.com

http://www.emilypost.com

http://en.wikipedia.org

http://www.etiquettehell.com

https://news.cgtn.com/news

https://www.qinxue365.com
http://en.shanximuseum.com
http://www.theworldofchinese.com
https://sergeygreen.com
https://www.theserviette.com
http://us.cnn.com